MW00377401

Your Best is Yet to Come: Leveraging Your Past for a Better future

Stan J. Tharp, D. Min.

2018

TABLE OF CONTENTS

Note: All Biblical references are from the New American Standard Version of the Bible unless otherwise noted. The Lockman Foundation. Anaheim, California: Foundation Publications. 1995

INTRODUCTION: Before you get started

The title of this book can be true for you regardless of who you are. *Your best is yet to come.* However, it's not automatic, you must make choices.

I'm writing this from the perspective of someone who has chosen to believe in and follow Jesus Christ. I'm a Christian and I would remind fellow Christians, ultimately our best is yet to come. That ultimate and final best is called Heaven.

This truth is dealt with in the last chapter of this book. It should be enough to help transform the way Christians live until we get to Heaven.

To those reading this book who are not Christians, I believe your best can also be yet to come. Many of the principles in the Bible have practical benefit even if you aren't a Christian. For instance, *"Do unto others as you would have them do unto you"* is a teaching of Jesus (Luke 6: 31), but it is also a pretty effective relational ethic.

All of us can benefit by learning from the examples offered from the lives of people who lived the Bible

> *The Bible indicates that the right thoughts can be transformational! Begin by believing that "Your (my) best is yet to come!" Then begin to live what you are learning.*

narrative. This book follows three men and two women who leveraged their past for a better future. You **can** do the same.

For non-Christians, you can improve your future exponentially by deciding to follow Jesus Christ as your personal Lord and Savior. The choice is yours, if you're interested, check out the final page of this book.

If you don't, some of the thoughts and choices by the "heroes" in this book will be almost impossible without God's help. Still, you can benefit by following the righteous principles provided.

Regardless, ALL of us need to realize the power of our thoughts, which influence our attitudes, behaviors and feelings. The Bible indicates that the right thoughts can be transformational! Begin by believing that *"Your (my) best is yet to come!"*

> *"Do not be conformed to this world, but be transformed by the renewing of your mind, so that you may prove what the will of God is, that which is good and acceptable and perfect"* (Romans 12: 2).

CHAPTER ONE: A Biblical survey of the past, present and future.

Today, yesterday and tomorrow. We live in the context of time. How we view time and what we do with it has a significant impact on our lives. We are finite creatures created by an eternal God, destined for a glorious and timeless eternity called Heaven. Whether or not we arrive in Heaven is a matter of personal choice; how we live our lives until we arrive there is also largely up to us.

Many people struggle, feeling that undesirable aspects or painful parts of their lives are not their "fault." Some may argue that their lives are a function of what has happened to them that they did not choose; perhaps people did things to them, or their life is a consequence of events out of their control. While it is true that none of us chooses every event and outcome in our lives, all of us must choose how we will respond to what has happened.

How we respond to our past has a significant impact on our present and future. We can build on a positive past or squander it. We can overcome the pain others inflict on us, or we can remain emotionally wounded by it. We can

> *While it is true that none of us chooses every event and outcome in our lives, all of us must choose how we will respond to what has happened.*

learn and grow from our failures or continually repeat them or remain permanently defeated by them.

A Biblical view of our lives makes it clear: We may not have caused many things in our lives, but we are responsible for how we will respond to those things. God has given us the power to choose how the events of our past affect us. He is eager to heal us, help us and grow us forward for His glory and our gain.

The Bible provides us a healthy perspective to have about our past, our present and our future. We have a choice about the person we will be; we can also choose the kind of life we will live in light of what we've experienced.

Below is a brief survey of verses that mention our past, present and future, along with the practice or attitude the Bible teaches us to follow:

1. *"In the beginning God created the heavens and the earth"* (Genesis 1: 1).
   God is eternal, He can be trusted with your past, present and future.

2. *"Jesus Christ is the same yesterday, today and forever"* (Hebrews 13: 8).
   Despite the fluctuations of our past, present and future, Jesus is our constant. We can always turn to Him, He was with us, He is with us, He will be with us, He understands.

3. *"And you shall remember that you were a slave in the land of Egypt, and the Lord your God brought you out of there by His outstretched arm..."* (Deuteronomy 5: 15).

Once we are forgiven by God, former bondage to sin should only be remembered to prompt grateful devotion to Christ, not guilt or shame.

4. "...for I will forgive their iniquity, and their sins I will remember no more" (Jeremiah 31: 34b).
God chooses to forgive and forget your sins. To the best of your ability, choose to forget the sins God has forgiven you.

God has given us the power to choose how the events of our past affect us. He is eager to heal us, help us and grow us forward for His glory and our gain.

5. *"Do not call to mind the former things or ponder things of the past. Behold, I will do something new, now it will spring forth..."* (Isaiah 43: 18, 19).
Learn to let go of the past and not continue to 'mull it over' in your mind, so you don't miss the new things God has planned.

6. *"Remember what the Lord your God did to Miriam on the way as you came out of Egypt"* (Deuteronomy 24: 9). Miriam was temporarily stricken with leprosy for gossiping against Moses (God's chosen leader), and for criticizing him for having what some people refer to as an interracial marriage.

Humbly allow the mistakes and sins of other people to offer you a learning opportunity and spare you the personal pain they experienced. "Go to school" on their mistakes, so-to-speak.

7. *"Remember, do not forget how you provoked the Lord your God to wrath in the wilderness..."* (Deuteronomy 9: 7).
   To prevent a false sense of self-righteousness, remember your past sins so you will be humbly reminded that the good God does is because of His grace, not because you earned it.

8. *"We remember the fish which we used to eat free in Egypt, the cucumbers and the melons and the leeks and the onions and the garlic, but now our appetite is gone"* (Numbers 11: 5, 6).
   Don't mentally re-write your history and glorify the wrong parts of your past. (Read Exodus 2: 23-25, the Israelites didn't "feast" for free; they were slaves for 400 years, and Egypt oppressed them harshly.)

9. *"Remember this day in which you went out from Egypt, from the house of slavery, for by a powerful hand the Lord brought you out of this place..."* (Exodus 13: 3).
   Once you leave sin/bondage behind, remember it was God's power that helped you do so, don't return to it.

10. *"He has made His wonders to be remembered, the Lord is gracious and compassionate..."* (Psalm 111: 4).
Remember the great things God has done in the past to inspire confidence, worship and gratitude from you.

11. *"Let this be a sign to you, so that when your children ask later, saying 'What do these stones mean to you...So these stones shall become a memorial to the sons of Israel forever..."* (Joshua 4: 6, 7).
Remember God's works to create grateful, faith-building family legacies.

12. *"And you shall remember all the way which the Lord your God has led you in the wilderness these forty years, that He might humble you, testing you, to know what was in your heart, whether you would keep His commandments or not"* (Deuteronomy 8: 2).
All of us go through "wilderness seasons." Learn to see the value in what is behind you and remember the past and see how God was faithful to you, tested and grew you.

13. *"This is the day which the Lord has made, let us rejoice and be glad in it"* (Psalm 118: 24).
Learn to consider each day as a gift from God and live trusting Him completely. Don't waste your todays or tomorrows living in the past.

14. *"See, I have set before you today life and prosperity, and death and adversity; in that I command you today to love the Lord your God, to walk in His ways and to keep His commandments, statutes and judgements...So choose life in order that you may live, you and your descendants, by loving the Lord your God, by obeying His voice, and by holding fast to Him"* (Deuteronomy 30: 15,16...19,20).
Every day is a fresh opportunity to choose to follow God and His word. This leads to a righteous and blessed life. Daily, choose life

15. *"Therefore, just as the Holy Spirit says, 'Today if you hear His voice...'"* (Hebrews 3: 7).
Learn to listen for God's voice of direction, affirmation and conviction in your daily life...and obey.

Whether or not we arrive in Heaven is a matter of personal choice. How we live our lives until we arrive there is also largely up to us.

16. *"But encourage each other day after day, as long as it is still called today, so that none of you will be hardened by the deceitfulness of sin"* (Hebrews 3: 13).
Live each day (in the present moments) as an opportunity to add value and encouragement to the life of others.

17. *"Behold, now is the acceptable time, behold, now is the day of salvation"* (2 Corinthians 6: 2).
    Don't disregard your spiritual potential, live each day for Jesus, pursuing His purpose in and through your life.

18. *"Come now, you who say, 'Today or tomorrow we will go to such and such a city and engage in business and make a profit.' Yet you do not know what your life will be like tomorrow"* (James 4: 13, 14).
    Learn to hold life loosely; as we're told in Proverbs 3, trust in the Lord with all your heart (today), and He will direct your paths.

19. *"Forgetting what lies behind, reaching forward to what lies ahead, I press on toward the goal, for the prize of the upward call of God in Christ Jesus"* (Philippians 3: 13, 14).
    Letting go of the past is essential for being able to "reach ahead" to the good things God has in store in your future. (You can't hold more good things if your hands are full of past junk.)

20. *"Strength and dignity are her clothing (a woman who loves and fears God), and she smiles at the future"* (Proverbs 31: 25).
    Be a godly person who looks forward to the future with optimistic anticipation.

21. *"Know that wisdom is thus for your soul; If you find it, then there will be a future, and your hope will not be cut off"* (Proverbs 24: 14).
Follow Godly wisdom and you can look forward to the future with hope.

22. *"For I know the plans that I have for you, declares the Lord, plans for welfare and not for calamity to give you a future and a hope"* (Jeremiah 29: 11).
Be encouraged, live optimistically. When God thinks about your future, His plans for you are good.

23. *"In the future there is laid up for me the crown of righteousness, which the Lord, the righteous judge, will award to me on that day, and not only to me but also to all who have loved His appearing"* (2 Timothy 4: 8).
Live as though you are looking forward to the reward you have earned through the God-honoring life you have lived.

24. *"Things which eye has not seen, and ear has not heard, and which have not entered the heart of man, all that God has prepared for those who love Him"* (1 Corinthians 2: 9).
Live knowing someday, you will be in Heaven; a place which will surpass anything we could possibly imagine!

25. *"Nevertheless, do not rejoice in this, that the spirits are subject to you, but rejoice that your names are recorded in Heaven"* (Luke 10: 20).

    The day you accepted Christ as your savior, a "heavenly birth certificate" of sorts was completed for you; your name was written in the "book of life" (Revelation 20: 15). You were "born again" to a new identity, to eternal life. Your eternal, abundant life starts NOW. Don't wait until Heaven to live the life Jesus intended for you.

QUESTIONS ABOUT THE BIBLICAL VIEW OF THE PAST, PRESENT AND FUTURE:

1. Select three passages and ideas from the above list that are most encouraging and motivating to you. Discuss why.

2. Which passages are the most difficult for you to consistently apply? Why?

3. Offer/think about an experience in your own life that validates one of the passages and perspectives listed above.

4. The introduction claims that even a person who doesn't follow Christ can benefit from following many of the principles in this book that were modeled by Biblical heroes. Do you agree or disagree? Why?

NOTES, THOUGHTS AND INSIGHTS:

CHAPTER TWO: Lessons from the life of Peter. Don't let past failures hold you back.

One of the most common fears in life is the fear of failure. All of us have failed at one time or another. None of us like the feeling.

Some failures are painful, like taking a risk relationally, only to have it end in rejection, disappointment or heartbreak. Whether it comes from family members, a spouse, friends, co-workers or a romantic interest, relational failures and pain are some of the hardest to overcome.

> *Failure can be a learning experience from which we grow and gain as a person, or it can be immobilizing, we can withdraw and promise ourselves to avoid the pain and "never do that again."*

Some failures are embarrassing, like joining a team only to find we are not measuring up. We might fail to deliver in a clutch moment or our skills are lacking, and we find ourselves the player who plays the least.

Some failures cost us a lot. We "take a risk" in our work world and rather than reaping a reward, we pay a price. Perhaps the business venture fails, or we get demoted, or lose our job altogether. Most of us reading this can easily offer up our own examples of trying, failing, and regretting the consequences.

Failure can be a learning experience from which we grow and gain as a person, or it can be immobilizing; we can withdraw and promise ourselves to avoid the pain and "never do that again." The impact of failure on our lives is largely under our control. As painful as it can be, the ultimate result of our failures (even if they are primarily someone else's fault) is up to us. We can pay the painful price of progress and grow and "fail forward" or we can withdraw into what seems like a "safe place." However, such safety can come at the big price of isolation, missed opportunities and forfeited dreams. Choose not to pay that price, choose the path where your past failures will propel you forward.

No one had more reason to allow his failures to drive him into isolation and fear than the apostle Peter. He could easily have taken a "never again" protective attitude. Instead, he is an inspiring example of how failure can propel us forward and prove that "the best is yet to come."

Lessons from the life of Peter:

> "...And after about an hour had passed,
> another man began to insist, saying,
> 'Certainly this man also was with Him, for
> he is a Galilean too.'
>
> But Peter said, 'Man, I do not know what
> you are talking about.' And immediately,
> while he was still speaking, a cock crowed.
>
> And the Lord turned and looked at Peter.
> And Peter remembered the word of the
> Lord, how He had told him, 'Before the cock
> crows today, you will deny Me three times.'
>
> And he went out and wept bitterly."
> (Luke 22: 59-62).

Doctors are trained to notice things about people including subtle things others might miss. This skill helps them accurately diagnose disease and prescribe appropriate treatments. Noticing subtle important details is something that often sets doctors apart from others.

Of the four Gospel writers, Luke is the only one who noticed and included a key subtle detail of the account of Peter's denial of Jesus.

Of the four Gospel writers, one was a doctor. Luke is called the "beloved physician" (Colossians 4: 14). No doubt he was also a good physician. While he wasn't one of the twelve disciples, Luke meticulously recorded the Gospel details of the life of Christ. Of the four Gospel writers, Luke is the only one who noticed and included a key subtle detail of the account of Peter's denial of Jesus.

All four Gospels record Peter's denial of Jesus in the courtyard of Caiaphas the high priest. Each of them mentioned his three denials immediately followed by a rooster crowing, just as Jesus predicted would happen. Only Dr. Luke included one of the most heart-rending moments in Peter's epic failure of Jesus. Only Luke included the simple sentence, just after Peter's third profanity-laced denial and moments before the cock crowed: *"And the Lord turned and looked at Peter"* (Luke 22: 61).

Eye contact! Imagine the scene: Fear and chaos have hit like a storm. The panicked disciples saw their world turn upside down overnight. Hours before, they were celebrating the Passover with Jesus, now He was on trial surrounded by calls for His arrest and execution!

Peter refused to flee like some of the disciples did, he was too loyal for that. However, as he tried to hide in the troubled crowd, bystanders began to recognize him as being associated with the miracle-maker. Contrary to his bold claim to die for Jesus, fear filled Peter's heart. The danger was real, hatred filled the air, and Peter caved. Peter did the unthinkable; Peter denied that he even knew Jesus, not once, but three times. To add certainty to his lie, he added some profanity to make his feigned disdain for Jesus believable.

At the very moment he spoke his third denial, Jesus looked Peter in the eye! It must have been one of those soul-piercing looks. You know the kind of look; it usually comes from someone like a close friend, a lover, a teacher, pastor, a parent or spouse. It's the kind of look that only people close to you can give. It's the kind of look that is met with your eyes, and when your gazes lock, volumes are said, soul-deep, without saying a word.

Dr. Luke is the only gospel writer to include this telling detail in his account of Peter's betrayal. This is an essential detail that shows the degree of devastation that hit Peter "like a ton of bricks" and explains why "...He went out and wept bitterly." Jesus was there, Peter was there, Peter denied Jesus, and Jesus looked him right in the eye at the moment of his greatest failure. Their gazes locked, their souls connected, a horrific sense of shame must have overwhelmed Peter, and he went out and wept bitterly!

This isn't the only failure of Peter that is in the Bible. There are at least two others recorded for all Biblical readers to see.

This isn't the only failure of Peter that is in the Bible. There are at least two others recorded for all Biblical readers to see. On one occasion Peter was with the disciples in a storm-tossed boat that seemed about to capsize! As fear filled the hearts of the disciples, some of whom came from a commercial fishing background, they looked out on the water and thought they were seeing a ghost! There in the storm, they saw Jesus walking toward them on the turbulent sea. As they cried out in fear for their lives Jesus called to them to take courage and reassured them it was indeed him.

Peter was a bit impulsive, so it wasn't surprising to the others when he cried out, "Lord, if it is you, command me to come to you on the water" (Matthew 14: 28). No sooner did Peter utter those regrettable words that Jesus obliged with a one-word invitation: "Come!"

Not surprisingly, as quickly as Peter called out, as quickly as Jesus invited him to an "on-sea stroll" Peter obliged and got out of the boat! We don't know how far Peter got in his miraculous walk of obedience and short-lived courage. Matthew is the only Gospel writer who records Peter's walk, all the Gospel notes is that "Peter got out of the boat and walked on the water and came toward Jesus" (Matthew 14: 29).

Whatever excitement Peter felt quickly switched to anxiety as it must have dawned on him, "Wait a minute, I'm walking on water...very stormy water...and I can't do that!" Matthew tells us Peter was filled with fear when he saw the wind, and he began to sink. Thankfully, Peter cried out to Jesus, and as he was beginning to sink, Jesus reached out and saved him and helped him into the boat.

> *Peter's third embarrassing moment is also caught in New Testament lore. The moment started out not unlike the walking on water incident.*

What happened next tops off the whole embarrassing episode for poor Peter. Rather than saying something like "Nice try Peter...at least you got out of the boat," Jesus reprimanded him. Peter was met with words that must have made him feel small indeed, Jesus said *"Oh you of little faith, why did you doubt?"* (Matthew 14: 31). Only moments before, Peter took a courageous step out of the boat, surely to become a standout among the fearful disciples. Now, wet with waves of fear, Peter was helped into the boat with embarrassing words of failure. He took his place among eleven other disciples who went from saying "Why didn't I get out of the boat?" to "I'm glad I didn't try that!"

Peter's third embarrassing moment is also caught in New Testament lore. The moment started out not unlike the walking on water incident. Peter blurted something out that was met positively by Jesus.

It was during a conversation with just the thirteen of them, Jesus asked the disciples who people said He was. After hearing their replies, He asked, "But who do you say that I am?" Peter answered, "Thou are the Christ, the Son of the living God" (Matthew 16: 16). Jesus lauded Peter for his reply, blessed him and affirmed that it was a revelation from God Himself that Peter had discerned. Jesus went on with the famously affirming remark, "And I say to you that you are Peter, and upon this rock I will build my church; and the gates of Hades shall not overpower it" (Verse 18). Jesus also promised to give Peter and presumably the rest of the disciples the "Keys to the Kingdom!"

Peter must have thought "Wow, did you hear that!? I'd say Jesus REALLY liked THAT answer!" Whether or not this affirmation stoked Peter's ego, we can only speculate. However, whatever kudos he received were short lived. The very next passage recorded another conversation between Jesus and the twelve.

Perhaps emboldened by Jesus' earlier affirmation of his heavenly insights, Peter chastised Jesus when he began to foretell the details of His own death. The Bible says Peter took Jesus aside and corrected Him. Sadly, Peter illustrated to us that a little inflated ego can go a long way!

No sooner did Peter say to Jesus "God forbid it Lord! This shall never happen to you" that Jesus rebuked Peter with the humiliating words: "Get behind me Satan!" Jesus further called Peter a

> *Imagine not only the failures of Peter, but the shame that came with it. Each time he might have thought he was going to "look good" to Jesus and the other disciples, Peter ended up embarrassed.*

"stumbling block" and accused him of promoting his own personal agenda (Matthew 16: 23).

On all three occasions Peter went from a high moment to humiliation. He boasted he would die for Jesus then denied him three times. He had the boldness to get out of the boat and step onto a storm-tossed sea then sank a few steps later. He gave a God-inspired reply identifying Jesus as the Son of God, then got rebuked as though he was being used against Jesus by Satan himself.

Imagine not only Peter's failures but the shame that came with them. Each time he might have thought he was going to "look good" to Jesus and the other disciples, Peter ended up embarrassed.

It's one thing to fail when no one else knows about it. When our failures are private, we can often convince ourselves to try again. Embarrassing failures that others know about can be more debilitating. When our family, friends or co-workers know about how we fell short, such failure can defeat us, silence us and even convince us to quit.

> *Embarrassing moments coupled with meaningful failure can bring shame, inflame our insecurities and even wound our willingness to try again.*

No doubt, in reading this book, many will recall "embarrassing moments." When we reminisce, some such moments are more laughable than devastating; like dropping a lunch tray in the cafeteria or dubbing a drive off the first tee of a company golf outing. Embarrassing moments coupled with meaningful failure can bring shame, inflame our insecurities and even wound our willingness to try again.

Surely childhood and adolescent failures often plant the roots of life-long insecurities that can flare up at a moment's notice. Adult efforts met by failure can stunt our growth emotionally, relationally or professionally. Failure coupled with embarrassment is a powerful stifling force against hopes and dreams and the willingness to try again.

We can only speculate how many careers were thwarted because of an unwillingness to risk failure (again); how many friendships never began or loves were lost for fear of being hurt (again); how many marriages stagnated for fear of awkward conversations (again); how many people abandoned dreams of who they hoped to become or what great goals stopped short of coming true in order to avoid disappointment (again).

Thankfully, we have an example to learn from in overcoming failure and shame. Peter, once a common fisherman became one of Jesus' closest friends, a chosen disciple, author of two books of the New Testament, and a founding father of Christianity and the early church. This is the same man whose failures have been recorded and re-read throughout two thousand years of history. His were no small "mess-ups."

Peter failed big! He failed publicly; he failed often, and his embarrassing failures are recorded in the Bible like none of the other disciples. Thinking about Peter's failures, the phrase "three strikes and you're out" comes to mind. Yet this person who some might see as a failure is also a hero. Peter refused to let failure define him or stop him.

Let's illustrate this exemplary trait about Peter. As you are reading this book, answer a quick quiz: "Jesus had twelve disciples, from memory, name them." (Pause take 60 seconds and see if you can pass this simple test.) Chances are high, you can't name all twelve. You probably got

Peter, James and John...maybe Andrew and Thomas and Judas, but all twelve? Nope. (For the other six, go ahead, read Matthew 10: 2-4).

Peter could have let his embarrassing public failures shame him into obscurity. He could have withdrawn in insecurity and lived in the risk-free safety of anonymity. He could have lived a devout, un-noticed life. *The point is that Peter stayed bold. Peter stayed willing to risk. Peter didn't allow failure to embarrass him into the safe shadows of discipleship.*

The lesson of Peter is not how to attain notoriety in Jesus' name. Most devout followers of Christ don't achieve notoriety or fame; surely this kind of recognition was not the goal of "no-name"

Peter failed big! He failed publicly; he failed often, and his embarrassing failures are recorded in the Bible like none of the other disciples.

disciples like Bartholomew and Thaddaeus. The lesson of Peter is that he didn't let failure define him. Failure didn't hold him back or keep him from trying again. Failure didn't stifle his growth from becoming all God wanted him to be. Failure didn't keep him from taking another risk and trying again.

How about you? What role does failure play in your life? We're not talking about the everyday, inconsequential variety of failure.

Most of our failures are relatively small and seemingly insignificant like failing to be courteous to an elderly person needing help with a door. At the hurried moment you rushed by them rather than assisting them, you failed to be the best version of you that you could be.

Failures can also be embarrassing in relatively harmless ways; like when you are trying to carry your laptop along with a handful of reports, and a Grande latte into the conference room, and you accidentally spill it all over yourself! These failures may embarrass us or be disappointing, but they don't realistically harm the bigger picture of our lives or who we are. Spilled lattes don't permanently damage our self-esteem or thwart our career path, and occasional unnoticed rude behavior is disappointing but not devastating.

How about you and your BIG failures, both public and private? Do they define and limit you? Do they haunt and bother you? Are there risks you are unwilling to take for fear of failure? Would you rather live with the disappointment of not trying rather than the pain of trying and failing again? Have you "been there done that" and vowed to never set yourself up like that again?

Are there risks you are unwilling to take for fear of failure? Would you rather live with the disappointment of not trying rather than the pain of trying and failing again?

Such fear and apprehension are understandable. The Bible tells us that "Hope deferred makes the heart sick, but desire fulfilled is a tree of life" (Proverbs 13: 12). People can only handle so much "deferred hope" until the pain takes over. We can only get our hopes up falsely so often that heartsickness says, "Enough! Don't risk such failure again."

Had Peter followed his fear from failure he certainly wouldn't have become the person we know him to be. Peter overcame failure and continued growing into the person and future God intended for him. As John Maxwell says in his book *Failing Forward, Turning Mistakes into Stepping Stones for Success*, "When it comes down to it, I know of only one factor that separates those who consistently shine from those who don't; the difference between average people and achieving people is their perception of a response to failure. Nothing else has the same kind of impact on people's ability to achieve and to accomplish whatever their minds and hearts desire."[1] An examination of Peter's life speaks to our own. None of us is immune to failure. God will use our failures to grow us forward, if we let Him. Our response to our failures during our failures is a key.

We can learn a few lessons from Peter.

First, *a long personal talk with Jesus seemed to help a great deal.* John records this conversation in the last chapter of his gospel (John 21: 15-23). The setting is a seaside stroll with Jesus, Peter and John shortly after Jesus resurrected. Jesus asked Peter three times, "Peter, do you love me?" The Bible says Peter was grieved when Jesus persisted in asking this question three times. Each time Peter insisted on his love for Christ. No doubt, Peter

---

[1] Goodreads. Online. "Failing Forward, How to Make the Most of Your Mistakes" John Maxwell, 2007. Thomas Nelson Publishers.

shamefully recalled his three courtyard denials of Jesus for every time he was asked, "Do you love me?"

In this talk with Jesus, something great obviously happened. Peter and Jesus came to terms with his failure. It's as though Jesus gave Peter the feeling, "You may have failed in the courtyard of the high priest, but I'd choose you all over again!" Their relationship was restored, and Peter was once again reminded that Jesus had a purpose for his life. *Peter's past failures would not define his future.*

> *Have a talk with Jesus. Tell him about your failure and your feelings. Ask Him for a clear, fresh vision of who He wants you to be, the purpose He has for you, and ask for the ability to move on.*

Learn from Peter. Accept the grace to move forward away from your past failures. Too many people can't forgive themselves for their failures. Too often, we shamefully accept that our failures define us and dictate our potential. Have a talk with Jesus. Tell him about your failures and your feelings. Ask Him for a clear, fresh vision of who He wants you to be, the purpose He has for you, and ask for the ability to move on.

Second: *Peter let the hope of a resurrected Christ give him confidence in new beginnings!* In John 20: 4-10, we read of the resurrection of Jesus. Peter and John heard rumors of an empty tomb; they ran to see for themselves, John stopped outside the tomb and looked in. Peter burst right into the tomb, eager and hope-filled to see the empty tomb for himself.

Jesus rose to new life, eternal life. Peter, John, and eventually the other disciples discovered this. *The resurrection of Jesus brings hope to a new level.* The empty tomb makes hope an unshakeable quality for those who follow Christ. By rising from the grave, Jesus became the champion of new beginnings. His followers were meant to be no less!

Peter's new beginning started in the first chapters of the book of Acts. After Jesus ascended to Heaven the disciples were confused as to what was next. The Bible tells us in Acts 1:15 "And at this time Peter stood up in the midst of the brethren, a gathering of about 120 persons, and said...."

> *By rising from the grave, Jesus became the champion of new beginnings. His followers were meant to be no less!*

Peter took his stand! What a change! Weeks before at the trial of Jesus, Peter was cowering in fear. After the hope of a resurrected Christ and a personal talk with Jesus, Peter chose confidence. After being filled with the Holy Spirit in Acts 2, the Bible again tells us in Acts 2: 14 *"Peter, taking his stand with the eleven raised his voice and declared...."* That day Peter preached a sermon that prompted over 3,000 people to follow Christ. He also stepped into a position of leadership of the New Testament church that he would maintain his whole life.

The resurrection of Jesus brings us the hope of starting over, of new beginnings. *Settle for nothing less in your life. Prayerfully ask for the wisdom, courage and grace to start over. Learn the lessons your failures have to offer you.* Ask the Holy Spirit to fill and empower you for the life Christ intends for you to live. Then humbly choose to have the courage to dream again, to try again.

Finally: *Regarding your experiences in life (failures or otherwise), choose your internal responses.* Peter chose his attitude toward adversity that sometimes results in failure. In one of the letters he wrote, he encouraged his readers to greatly rejoice, *"even though now for a little while, if necessary, you have been distressed by various trials..."* (1 Peter 1: 6-9). Peter wrote as a mature, confident Christian. He didn't write as an insecure failure. On the contrary, Peter learned that trials come to refine us not defeat us. We can use past failures to propel us forward. Your response to your failures is truly your choice.

Peter also chose to find his worth and the basis for his self-esteem in Christ. He reminded his readers "That you were not redeemed with perishable things like silver or gold...but with the precious blood of Christ..." (1 Peter 1: 18, 19). Peter realized that if God decided it was worth sacrificing his son Jesus to redeem Peter (and all who believe in Christ), who was he to argue? Peter would no longer languish in insecurity and unworthiness, he chose to accept his precious sense of worth in God's eyes. Doing so puts failure into perspective. God is a God of grace and power. He can forgive our failures and use them to teach and shape us; He can then empower us for future good.

> On the contrary, Peter learned that trials come to refine us not defeat us. We can use past failures to propel us forward. Your response to your failures is truly your choice.

All of us fail. The key is what you will do in response? What do you tell yourself? Who do you believe yourself to be? What are the limits on you considering your failures? Learn to let past failures propel you forward. Forgive yourself, forgive others and ask God for the grace to learn and then try again.

QUESTIONS FROM THE LIFE OF PETER:

1. What range of emotions do you suppose Peter experienced in each of the failures mentioned in the Bible?

    A. Sinking (rather than walking) on water.

    B. Being praised and shortly afterward being rebuked by Jesus.

    C. Denying Christ in the courtyard of the high priest.

2. How can we have a "talk with Jesus" about our embarrassing/shameful failures that could help us recover from them and regain confidence like Peter did?

3. What failure(s) in your past threaten your confidence, self-esteem or willingness to "try again?"

NOTES, THOUGHTS AND INSIGHTS:

CHAPTER THREE: Lessons from the life of Esther. Be the unlikely, unexpected success.

Expectations play a big part in life. When we have positive expectations that are met, we're pleased. If unmet, we're disappointed.

Beyond what we expect of ourselves, we place expectations on other people. When people meet our expectations, it reinforces our trust in and opinion of them.

People also have expectations of us. What people expect of us, and how

> *What people expect of us and how those expectations are communicated can have a powerful influence on our self-image and our behavior.*

those expectations are communicated can have a powerful influence on our self-image and our behavior. Generally, we like to meet the expectations of others; their expectations can be a strong motivating or demotivating force in our lives.

Esther shows us how to thrive even when no one else expects it of you. She could have easily "sunk" to the level of what was expected of her, but she rose above and beyond the expectations of those around her.

Learn how to thrive, regardless if prevailing attitudes are "No one like you has ever done that before..."

Lessons from the life of Esther.

> *"Now there was a Jew in Susa, the capital whose name was Mordecai, the son of Jair, the son of Shimei, the son of Kish, a Benjaminite, who had been taken into exile from Jerusalem with the captives who had been exiled with Jeconiah the king of Judah, whom Nebuchadnezzar the king of Babylon had exiled.*
>
> *And he was bringing up Hadassah, that is Esther, his uncle's daughter, for she had neither father nor mother..."* (Esther 2: 5-7).

The story of Esther took place during the reign of King Ahasuerus (Xerxes was his Greek name). His was a massive, powerful empire, spanning over 127 provinces stretching from India to Ethiopia. His queen, Vashti, had just disobeyed his command to come and pose for him and his banquet guests, displaying her famous beauty.

She mustered the courage to refuse indulging his lustful arrogance and paid the price.

This rejection threw the somewhat impulsive king into a rage: *"Then the king became very angry and his wrath burned within him"* (Esther 1: 12.) He consulted with his seven nobles who took up with his offense on behalf of all men in Persia. They affirmed his concerns in their male-dominated culture and asked for her removal as queen:

36

*"For the queen's conduct will become
known to all the women causing them to
look with contempt on their husbands by
saying, 'King Ahasuerus commanded Queen
Vashti to be brought in to his presence, but
she did not come.' And this day the ladies of
Persia and Media who have heard of the
queen's conduct will speak in the same way
to all the king's princes, and there will be
plenty of contempt and anger..."*
(Esther 1: 17, 18).

Poor Vashti. The king had been hosting a lavish party for seven days. The Bible notes he was "merry with wine" and in the mood to show off his beautiful queen. Such hedonistic pleasure surely sickened Vashti. No doubt, this wasn't the first time her king made her feel more like a lustful possession than a beloved queen. She mustered the courage to refuse indulging his lustful arrogance and paid the price.

Sometime later, the Bible notes the king must have "come to his senses" and realized what he had done; he dethroned his beautiful queen. Not willing for the impulsive king to be sad for long (one never knew what the king's bad mood could generate), his attendants suggested an empire-wide search be made for the most beautiful virgin to be selected to replace Vashti in his royal harem. The self-absorbed king was delighted and agreed!

Esther (also known as Hadassah) was one of the beautiful young virgins taken into custody for a possible spot in the king's harem, and perhaps, to be selected as his queen.

The program of preparation was twelve months long. Esther immediately caught the attention of Hegai, the overseer of the harem. He assigned her seven female attendants, placed her in "the best place in the harem," and began her year-long diet and beauty program (see Esther 2: 8-14). The selection ritual culminated in each candidate leaving the preparation harem to spend a night with the king. Then they return to a secondary harem to await the king's pleasure.

The Bible says *"the king loved Esther more than all the women, and she found favor and kindness with him more than all the virgins, so that he set the royal crown on her head and made her queen instead of Vashti..."* (Esther 2: 17).

Esther inspires anyone, especially any woman, to not let "the way things have always been" dictate "the way things will be."

The magnitude of what was about to happen with Esther escapes our modern understanding. The Jewish people had been living as conquered exiles for centuries; first by the Babylonians, then (when Persia conquered Babylon) by the Persians. They lived at the mercy of warrior empires. Esther (Hadassah) was a Jewish orphan, and she was about to become the most powerful and influential woman in Persia.

Surely, Esther realized that no one like her had ever become queen. None of the Jewish women in her ancestry had ever held such a position of significance. Esther inspires anyone, especially any woman, to not let "the way things have always been" dictate "the way things will be."

Just because "no one like you has ever done that before" wasn't reason for Esther to not step into her position as Queen of Persia. She did and soon began to use her influence. Her older cousin (and guardian) Mordecai soon informed the young queen of an assassination plot against the king. She told the king, the plot was discovered, and her credibility increased (Esther 2: 21-23).

About this time, a new political appointee of the king named Haman developed a hatred for the Jews; and specifically, for Esther's cousin Mordecai. Haman convinced the king to adopt a plan to launch a genocide and literally destroy the Jewish race scattered throughout the empire. As news of this plan spread among the Jews and finally to Mordecai and Esther, they wept with great anguish.

Mordecai appealed to Esther, who yet until this time had not told the king that she was Jewish. Faced with the temptation to keep her identity hidden while countless Jews died, Esther faced a decision. Mordecai appealed to his now royal cousin. Mordecai begged her not to stay silent any longer, but to make her voice known to the king. If she remained silent, Mordecai noted her people would perish. His timeless words moved the young queen from caution to courage: *"And who knows whether you have attained royalty for such a time as this?" (Esther 4: 14)*

Esther stood at a formidable crossroad of decision; she could remain silent about her identity and watch countless victims die, or she could risk it all and try to make a difference. Great deeds are like that; seldom are they done without someone willing to pay a price. Abraham Lincoln paid the ultimate personal price to break the bonds of slavery on an entire nation. Dr. Martin Luther King Jr. paid that same ultimate price to further dissolve the lingering systemic injustices that a civil war left unfinished.

First, she demonstrated the importance of spiritual support and guidance as she asked Mordecai to mobilize the local Jewish community to fast and pray.

Esther had the ultimate dream of every woman of her time, she was the "Queen of Persia." She had wealth, fame, power, and a life of decadent luxury. All she needed to do to sustain it was live in pleasing harmony with the king. Why should she risk all that, as well as face the possibility of imprisonment, torture or even death, to save a people she now only anonymously shared an unremarkable heritage of exile with?

The story of Esther speaks courage to all of us, but especially to women, young women of today who are open to the truths of scripture. NEVER underestimate what God can do through a woman called, empowered and yielded to Him. Listen to the amazing courage and spiritual fortitude of this young exile-queen as she replied to Mordecai's earlier plea:

"Then Esther told them to reply to Mordecai, 'go assemble all the Jews who are found in Susa, and fast for me: do not eat or drink for three days, night or day. I and my maidens also will fast in the same way. And thus, I will go in to the king, which is not according to the law; and if I perish, I perish" (Esther 4: 16).

This must be one of the most under-rated and inspiring, courageous, selfless decisions of all human history! Esther accepted the challenge to risk her life and position to save a nation, acknowledging that God may very well have placed her as Queen of Persia "for such a time as this."

First, she demonstrated the importance of spiritual support and guidance as she asked Mordecai to mobilize the local Jewish community to fast and pray. She also asked her immediate circle of companions to do the same. Then she resolved that she would indeed risk

> *Esther has accepted the challenge to risk her life and position to save a nation, acknowledging that God may very well have placed her as Queen of Persia "for such a time as this."*

it all and go to the king. It is important to understand that ancient cultures were different than today. Indeed, she was the king's wife (the queen among his many wives), but she didn't have unfettered access to her husband. Even she was required to follow protocol to enter his presence for a discussion about governance.

Suspicion ran high in ancient governments; rulers gained power by force and typically lost it the same way, either through military defeat or assassination. Ultimately, no one was trusted by a monarch. King Herod at the time of Christ even had two of his own sons killed whom he thought were planning a coup. As such, everyone, including the king's wife, must follow the laws of access to the king.

Esther was aware of this. She decided she would approach the king in this emergency even in defiance of protocol. Esther would expose her previously undisclosed nationality, risk all the rights and privileges of being queen, AND risk her life. She summarized her amazing courage with *"...and if I perish, I perish"* (Esther 4: 16).

The outcome of her courage is fascinating. Not only did she save a nation, she also initiated a most cunning plan to expose and depose the ruthless Haman that had infiltrated the King's most intimate circle of influence. Esther reached unparalleled fame in the Persian Empire, even to the point of establishing protective laws for the Jews throughout Persia: *"And the command of Esther established these customs for Purim, and it was written in the book."* (Esther 9: 32)

Further, Mordecai, her cousin and Godly advisor was placed second-in-command in Persia. He too became an exemplary leader: *"For Mordecai the Jew was second only to King Ahasuerus and great among the Jews, and in favor with the multitude of his kinsmen, one who sought the good of his people and one who spoke for the welfare of his whole nation"* (Esther 10: 3).

Added to all this drama is the fact that young Esther was unprepared and unexpecting of such a position of power, wealth and influence. Whether anyone said it to her, surely many thought "No one like you has ever done this before; they have never been chosen to appear before the king. They have never been selected queen. They have never used such influence to risk everything to save a nation, and as a result, rise to a position of even greater power." Esther was a common woman of uncommon courage with an uncommon vision for what is possible in a life that looks beyond risks and is fully surrendered to the will of God.

> *Her cousin Mordecai challenged her to "step up" at this dangerous time and see her blessing of being queen as having a purpose.*

Granted, Esther was born with exceptional beauty. But don't let this unearned advantage minimize what she chose; she still had to make a choice, and she chose to use her blessing for a greater purpose. She also chose to lay aside any hindering sense of unworthiness, or "who me?" and confidently step into what God wanted her to do.

Esther's story speaks especially loud and clear to women, and most specifically to young women: be willing to take courageous risks for the right reasons, at the right moments in time. Such "moments" are rarely announced or anticipated. A crisis in the royal court (Queen Vashti dishonors the king) turned into a wildly improbable opportunity for Esther; she was invited to audition for a place in the king's harem and a long shot at becoming queen.

How about you? You may see yourself as an ordinary person, but you too are capable of uncommon courage and the ability to live a life of significance. You can pursue the purpose behind the blessings in your life.

But don't let this unearned advantage minimize what she chose; she still had to make a choice, and she chose to use her blessing for a greater purpose.

Most of us lack any outstanding distinction, we are common. Most of us won't do heroic deeds that are recorded and read for thousands of years. However, common doesn't mean incapable. Common doesn't mean without purpose or potential. As life presents opportunities that may seem beyond you, don't accept the idea that "no one like me has ever done this before" and passively decide to "sit this one (opportunity) out."

This isn't an invitation to irresponsible fantasy. As much as I might enjoy it, there is just no way I'm ever going to earn a living with anything to do with a sports ball (golf, basketball, baseball, football, soccer). At my best, I was only a recreational, "pick-up game" kind of athlete. I never need to wonder if God is going to use me in the world of sports in an unexpected way. Of course, add to this that my physical prime was decades ago…it's never going to happen!

However, being realistic about our limitations doesn't mean we should underestimate our potential. As a believer, you have "Christ within you, the hope of glory" (Colossians 1: 27). This is a powerful truth and compelling promise. God doesn't "save us" just to keep us from Hell. God saved us to redeem us for Heaven and to fulfill His purpose through us on Earth:

> *"For by grace you have been saved through faith; and that not of yourselves, it is the gift of God...for we are His workmanship, created in Christ Jesus for good works, **which God prepared beforehand**, that we should walk in them." (Ephesians 2: 8, 10)*

There are "God-prepared" good works that He wants you and only you to do. Imagine our regret when someday we may realize how many of those good works went undone due to distraction, and worse, due to our self-imposed sense of inadequacy or a hindering sense of fear. Everyone has an excuse why NOT to try. Some excuses are more convincing and debilitating than others. What are yours? What opportunities have you passed by just because you convinced yourself you

> *There are "God-prepared" good works that He wants you to and only you to do. Imagine our regret when someday we may realize how many of those good works went undone due to distraction, and worse, due to our self-imposed sense of inadequacy or a hindering sense of fear.*

couldn't, shouldn't, or people like you are just kidding themselves to try, or maybe you just couldn't muster up the courage?

We can learn a few lessons from the life of Esther.

In Esther we see an "ordinary" person displaying extraordinary courage and exemplary wisdom. Yes, Esther became queen, but before her external circumstances changed, she was just a girl of the exile living as a defeated foreigner in Persia. Esther was willing to make decisions and live beyond her history, her identity, and the expectations of others.

First, *live beyond your history*. Hopefully your past has been perfect supportive preparation for your future. However, if it is, you are surely in the minority of people. For most of us our past is a mixed bag, containing both blessings and curses. There are probably some great advantages in your past, that prepared you for your "now," but there are also likely some great setbacks, limitations or struggles.

You have decisions to make. You can choose to let your past setbacks hinder your future OR, *you can decide that what is behind you doesn't need to negatively determine what you will do or who you will be.*

Second, *live beyond your current identity*. Our self-concept begins to be formed in our infancy. We have a variety of inputs that guide this process, here are just a few: family experiences and attitudes about us; personal experiences and our own self-talk; and the attitudes of others toward us (whether they are stated or just perceived).

None of us have all positive inputs to the process of establishing our sense of self-esteem. Our lives are a mixture of positives and negatives from others, within ourselves, and in the world around us. Some negative experiences and feedback are intentionally harsh and hurtful, critical and belittling. Other negative inputs are indirect or subtle, but we sense them just the same.

Hopefully, your overall sense of self-concept is positive; you feel capable for life and are eager and optimistic about the future and your abilities to thrive.

> *You can choose to see who you are as a work-in-process rather than a permanent definition (and limitation) of who you are, who you will be, and what you are capable of.*

However, you may be on the other end of the continuum. You may be among those who wrestle daily with feelings of inadequacy and worthlessness. For you hope may be infrequent and your confidence is limited or non-existent. Depending on where a person is on this continuum largely determines their optimistic sense of engagement with the challenges and opportunities of life or their sense of withdrawal and pre-determined defeat.

Esther could have yielded to insecurity and never attempted to audition for the king's harem, much less to be queen. She could have told herself a true yet limiting statement: "No one like me has ever done this before...who am I kidding?" Instead, Esther courageously stepped out of any insecurity of her identity and took the risk to believe she could become someone more than she or anyone else previously believed she could be.

Like Esther, you can choose to see who you are as a work-in-process rather than a permanent definition (and limitation) of who you are, who you will be, and what you are capable of. In reading Esther's story, we watch an amazing transformation in a young woman willing to courageously believe and take risks. The story of Esther began with a lowly girl living in exile in a foreign land. It ended with Esther as a courageous queen who saved an entire nation and lived in a position of influence.

Determine that with God's help you will see yourself as a work-in-process, not a culmination of past failures. Choose to add courage and confidence to your insecurity. Perhaps you should go for that education, set some goals, optimistically equip yourself for what might be ahead. Prayerfully ask God for a more possibility-oriented sense of who you are and what you are capable of. If necessary, ask Him for a redemptive re-interpretation of your past. (For more on reinterpreting your past, find the book *Unstuck* available on Amazon by this author).

> *Refuse to shrink back from God's design and desire for your life. Say yes, believe you were created, blessed and positioned "for such a time as this." Your best is yet to come!*

Third, *look for and live out the purpose God has in your blessings.* God obviously blessed Esther with a life of amazing wealth and privilege for a reason. God raised her up as queen "for such a time as this." It was time for Esther to live out God's purpose, not just her own.

Think of all the blessings in your life. We all have some, most of us have many. What purpose does God have for bestowing and sustaining those blessings in your life? Realize the truth of Ephesians 2: 10 applies to you, He has *"Good works that He has prepared beforehand (prior to you becoming a Christian) that He wants you to do."* The blessings in your life are likely to be tools or resources to help you accomplish the good works that God has chosen for you so walk in them. Get started.

Finally, *Choose courage.* All of us have reason to yield our dreams and potential to insecurity, to the low expectations of others, and to past limiting failures and identities. Be like Esther. Refuse to shrink back from God's design and desire for your life. Say yes! Believe you were created, blessed and positioned "for such a time as this." Your best is yet to come!

QUESTIONS FROM THE LIFE OF ESTHER:

1. As a young woman of a conquered nation living in exile, Esther had little observable reason for a hopeful future. What are some situations in your own past that could reinforce insecurity or doubt about you or your future?

2. Esther chose a courageous course of action to save the Jews. She accepted the challenge that God had blessed her "for such a time as this." What are some of the obvious ways you have been blessed in your life?

3. If you could make a positive difference for some cause, what would it be? If you could make a positive impact for others in need, who might that be? How might this be part of the "Good works which God prepared beforehand "that He wants you to pursue in your life? (Ephesians 2: 8-10).

NOTES, THOUGHTS AND INSIGHTS:

CHAPTER FOUR: Lessons from the life of Joseph. Don't let what others did to you control your future.

Much of what happens to us in life is out of our control. If good things happen to us and we had nothing to do with it, we call ourselves "lucky, or blessed." If bad things happen, it's the reverse.

Much of what happens to us is a result of the actions of other people. When offenses are minor (like a rude driver cutting us off in traffic) we easily dismiss their bad behavior. If the offense is significantly damaging or abusive, recovery is more complicated and difficult. If they are a stranger to us, the dismissal is usually easier to do. If we have a relationship with the offender, their undesirable deed can be more difficult to overcome or forget. The thought that they may have committed the offense knowingly, or even worse, intentionally adds the dimension of being hurt. We can wonder, "How could they do that to me? Why did they do that to me?"

> ...It is important that we learn how to minimize the length and scope of the damage others have done to us.

Whether offenses against us are great or small, intentional or accidental by someone close to us or a total stranger, it is important that we learn how to minimize the length and scope of the damage others have done to us. Unfortunately, many reading this are living in the shadows of someone else's past offenses against them. Perhaps the abuse or wrong treatment is long-gone, or perhaps it is ongoing in a current relationship.

Their bad treatment of you, whether it be rudeness, abuse, injustice, neglect or rejection can cause bad after-effects. Lingering feelings of hurt, anger, or insecurity can cause ongoing internal struggles long after the offense has ceased, if we let it.

Perhaps no one knows about suffering personal injustice at the hands of loved ones better than Joseph; surely no one is a better example of how to overcome it.

Learn how to not let your future be controlled by what others did to you.

Lessons from the life of Joseph:

"So, it came about, when Joseph reached his brothers, that they stripped Joseph of his tunic, the varicolored tunic that was on him; and they took him and threw him into the pit.

Then some Midianite traders passed by, so they pulled him up and lifted Joseph out of the pit and sold him to the Ishmaelites for twenty shekels of silver. Thus, they brought Joseph into Egypt" (Genesis 37: 23, 28).

The most potentially devastating soul-wounds we can experience are typically from people who are close to us. When someone like a family member, spouse, friend or co-worker takes advantage of us, abuses us or betrays us their familiarity adds "how COULD they" to our pain. Unfortunately, you may also know this first-hand as you live in the recent or long-past yet lingering after-math of someone else's sins against you. No-one knows what this is like more than Joseph.

Joseph was the second youngest of the twelve sons of Jacob. Sibling rivalry can be significant in a large family. In Joseph's family it was aggravated by the fact that he was clearly Jacob's favorite. The Bible notes this: *"Now Israel (another name for Jacob) loved Joseph more than all his sons, because he was the son of his old age; and he made him a varicolored tunic"* (Genesis 37: 3).

It was Joseph, not Jacob's youngest son Benjamin who was noted as his favorite. We can only speculate reasons; perhaps Jacob harbored negative feelings about Benjamin because his beloved wife Rachel died in giving birth to Benjamin. Whatever the reasons, Joseph was his father's favorite son.

> *Imagine Joseph's panic-level fear. Imagine the horror of being a slave on his way to parts unknown in the Egyptian empire! Imagine the pain of this betrayal. Imagine how hurt he would be knowing his ten brothers did this to him!*

Joseph's brothers sold him into slavery when he was just seventeen years old (Genesis 37: 2). Dirty deeds often don't just happen one at a time; this is true in the case with Joseph's brothers. After selling their brother into slavery, they told their grieving father an elaborate lie to cover their treachery. They took the symbol of their father's favoritism, Joseph's multi-colored coat, and dipped it in goat's blood, and convinced Jacob that their resented brother was killed by a wild animal.

Imagine their cold-hearted deceit. These ten brothers (Benjamin was not involved) lied to their dad, and then watched him go through a horrible grieving process for Joseph, knowing all along their brother was alive and now a slave because of their doing.

To call this sibling rivalry is to sugar-coat their wrong. This is unthinkably cruel abuse at the hands of his own family! Joseph was now someone else's property, a common slave, on his way to "Who knows where?" in Egypt.

Imagine Joseph's panic-level fear. Imagine the horror of being a slave on his way to parts unknown in the Egyptian empire! Imagine the pain of this betrayal. Imagine how hurt he would be knowing that his ten brothers did this to him!

Scripture is silent on the abuses Joseph may have endured at the hand of the Midianites as they travelled the long journey to Egypt. We only know that upon arrival, *"...the Midianites sold him in Egypt to Potiphar, Pharaoh's officer, the captain of the bodyguard"* (Genesis 37: 36).

The story of Joseph does not have a quick "happily ever after" resolution; seventeen-year-old Joseph would remain a slave until he was thirty years old! While details are limited, we do know that Joseph was a trustworthy slave. He earned a position of trust from his master Potiphar.

> *Once back in jail, Joseph refused to become a resentful reaction to injustice. His positive and trustworthy attitude could not be stifled.*

However, Potiphar's own wife wrongly accused Joseph of trying to take advantage of her. Once again, poor Joseph found himself the victim of injustice and he was unfairly sent back to prison (Genesis 39: 20).

Once back in jail, Joseph refused to become a resentful reaction to injustice. His positive and trustworthy attitude could not be stifled, and Joseph was placed into a position of favor while in jail. The chief jailer put Joseph over all the king's prisoners and *"whatever he did, the Lord made to prosper"* (Genesis 39: 23).

While serving in the jail, Joseph interpreted the dreams of two of the king's prisoners, the cupbearer and the baker. Since the dream of the cupbearer meant he would be restored to his position in the royal court, Joseph asked the cupbearer to remember him to Pharaoh when the interpretation of the dream came true. Sadly, once again Joseph's hopes failed as *"the chief cupbearer did not remember Joseph but forgot him" (Genesis 40: 23).*

Two years passed before the cupbearer would remember Joseph. The king had a troubling dream no one could interpret, and the cupbearer finally told Pharaoh about Joseph. Joseph was brought before Pharaoh and gave the accurate interpretation along with an appropriate solution to address the seven-year famine foretold in the dream.

Joseph's roller-coaster life of favor and injustice continued for thirteen years.

Joseph was once again raised to a position of favor, this time by Pharaoh. He was appointed as the number two leader in the entire Egyptian empire! (Genesis 41: 40).

Joseph's roller-coaster life of favor and injustice continued for thirteen years. It wasn't until Joseph hit "the big 3-0" that he finally left a life of slavery for good. Imagine the relief and disbelief! Finally, Joseph got his unjustly lost freedom back. Finally, Joseph felt a sense of purpose for his life. Finally, Joseph would begin to see his dreams come true...literally. As a teen, Joseph had a dream that his family would one day bow down and pay homage to him. For the amazing story, read Genesis 39: 5-8

In the meantime, Joseph's brothers continued extended family life with their father. Few details are recorded of Jacob's family during the time Joseph was living in slavery. The primary Biblical narrative shifted to Joseph during his years in Egypt. When his thirteen years of slavery ended, Joseph was promoted to be second in command to Pharaoh himself. He oversaw Egypt's food supply in preparation for a seven-year famine foretold in the dream he interpreted for Pharaoh. His Jewish family was beginning to feel the effects of the famine. Jacob sent his sons on a mission to buy food in Egypt. The Bible also recorded Jacob's apprehension in sending his youngest son Benjamin the only other son through his beloved wife Rachel. He was terrified of losing him as well:

"Now Jacob saw that there was grain in Egypt, and Jacob said to his sons, 'Why are you staring at one another?'

And he said, 'Behold, I have heard that there is grain in Egypt; go down there and buy some for us from that place, so that we may live and not die.'

Then ten brothers of Joseph went down to buy grain from Egypt. But Jacob did not send Joseph's brother Benjamin with his brothers, for he said, 'I am afraid that harm may befall him.'"

(Genesis 42: 1-4)

The story of Joseph raises the question, "What do you do when you suffer wrong from others?" This includes people close to you that you trusted (in his case, family) and people who had no reason to abuse or accuse you (like Potiphar's wife).

> Other people live in ongoing bitterness for what happened to them and they pay the perpetual price in their own lives, their relationships, choices, and internal state of well-being.

We tend to dismiss minor offenses. It is not uncommon to be cut off in traffic, or be treated rudely by a coworker, or even by a stranger. Such ordinary offenses simply blend in to the collective life memories that we soon forget. Often, such hurts eventually fade to a place we can't even recall them if we try.

This kind of forgetfulness can be healthy and serves as a bit of a mental defense mechanism. If remembering difficult, frustrating or painful experiences offers no practical benefit (lessons to learn or dangers to avoid) our mind eventually no longer expends the emotional or mental energy to keep them alive and typically just lets such memories fade. We can still recall the *feeling* of being mistreated, but the details just aren't worth the energy of maintaining.

On the other hand, major hurts, offenses or injustices are different. Most of us have some experience of significant, disruptive or lasting pain because of what someone else has done to us. Even reading that sentence will trigger memories for many. Things suffered at the hand of

59

another can wound us soul deep. Sometimes such wounds are accompanied by physical bruises; sometimes the wounds are unseen but just as real. Injustice can destroy our innocence and our ability to trust (imagine how defensive you'd be, being sold into slavery by your own brothers). Undeserved pain or betrayal can stay with us and cause struggles long after the events have ceased.

Many people find it difficult, if not impossible, not to be affected by what someone else has done to them. Try as they might, they can't forget what they suffered. Perhaps the betrayal or pain was so great that they live in constant lingering fear, insecurity or anger. Other people live in ongoing bitterness for what happened to them and they pay the perpetual price in their own lives, their relationships, choices, and internal state of well-being.

Many people have relational struggles as a lingering effect of how someone mistreated them. They get easily upset or depressed when dealing with people (especially difficult people.) Others find it hard to trust people even though they had nothing to do with past hurts.

We can find it hard to be optimistic or to trust God for our greater good, since He seemed to allow our past pain.

Some people have such a root of shame or insecurity within themselves because of what someone did to them in their past that it hinders most other relationships in their life. When such self-doubt is internalized it can hurt a person's ability to dream, to take healthy risks, and to become all they Ma

Often the injustice is in our past, but we must continue to be around that person making our feelings difficult to resolve. Perhaps the person is an unavoidable co-worker or boss; maybe the offender is your spouse or a family member. While you might be able to leave it in the past you keep being reminded of it during your ongoing dealings with the person.

When we can't escape what someone has done to us, it can create an internal sense of hopelessness, a cynical attitude or sense of depression. We can find it hard to be optimistic or to trust God for our greater good, since He seemed to allow our past pain.

Many people find themselves unable to process past injustice they have suffered, and they just stuff it or try to ignore the pain. While this occasionally works just leaving things alone can also allow a subtle and pervasive bitterness to grow. Ignoring what needs to be attended to can do more harm than good.

The Bible even warns us about the self-perpetuating damage of living in the shadow of someone else's sin against us: *"See to it that no one comes short of the grace of God; that no root of bitterness springing up causes trouble, and by it many be defiled..."* (Hebrews 12: 15). It has been said "bitterness and unforgiveness is the poison we drink hoping someone else will die."[2]

How about you? How have you handled the significant wrongs others have done to you? This isn't referring to the ordinary daily inconsiderate, rude or self-serving things

___

[2] Marianne Williamson. Brainy Quotes.com. Accessed August 21, 2018.

people do at your expense. How have you handled the "big hurts" done to you by others?

Hopefully such events are few and far between in your life. For most people this is true. However, many people find that one situation or problematic relationship can have an ongoing ripple effect on them, their lives, their decisions, and those around them.

Consider Joseph. He could easily have become a bitter mess filled with life-long hatred toward his brothers that spilled over onto his ongoing attitudes about people and life in general.

This isn't to suggest that you must keep major offenses at the forefront of your attention or as part of who you are.

Joseph could have inappropriately owned his brothers' selfishness and adopted an unworthy self-esteem under the guise of "I must be a horrible person for my own family to hate me so much."

Denial certainly isn't the answer either. Some people simply refuse to face the offenses that are behind them in hopes that they can somehow outrun them with an obsession with living for today or relentlessly pursing future dreams.

This isn't to suggest that you must keep major offenses at the forefront of your attention or as part of who you are. It is healthy to forgive and forget; it is just important to do so properly.

We can learn a few lessons from the life of Joseph. This raises the question, "How did Joseph do it?" How did young Joseph endure the horrible sins of his brothers and not allow it to damage the rest of his life? How did Joseph stay positive and hopeful?

First, *Joseph must have had a moment of decision in which he determined not to live as a reaction to what was done to him nor to repeat it in his own life.* I recall a conversation with my father when I was in my thirties. He grew up in a home devastated by his father's alcoholism. His parents' marriage ended, and his nine siblings scattered across the country each to process their pain in different ways.

Having a graduate degree in counseling and having sat with many people trying to sort out past pain, I asked him, "Dad, I'm thankful our family didn't resemble yours, how did you do it? How did you not pass along any of the abusive dysfunction you lived in?" My experience is that this is an exception and not the norm. Sadly, far too many people tend to repeat the pain they experience and regrettably inflict what they endured onto themselves and those they love.

> *Likewise, young Joseph must have had a soul-deep resolve that the sins of his brothers were not going to control who he became or how he would live.*

What my dad said reminds me of the kind of response Joseph might have given to a similar question. He said, "I just drew a line in the sand and determined that with God's help, I was NOT going to repeat the pain and sins I had to endure in my home as a child."

This isn't to suggest that a simple decision coupled with personal willpower can suffice in overcoming significant pain others have inflicted on us in the past. My dad followed his decision with a lifetime of applied determination to honor God in his family, his career, his church involvement, and his inner world. Thankfully for me, I did not experience a trans-generational repeat of what he grew up with.

Likewise, young Joseph must have had a soul-deep resolve that the sins of his brothers were not going to control who he became or how he would live. This is an amazing thought, especially since Joseph's brothers sold him into slavery and determined the undesirable external circumstances of his life from the age of seventeen until he reached thirty.

What his brothers did to him made Joseph a slave in his circumstances; BUT, what they did to him could not imprison Joseph in his soul! Joseph resolved to be free from dysfunctional reactions to their sin against him, even though he remained physically imprisoned because of them.

You may be forced to live in circumstances someone else imposed on you. Perhaps you are living in the strenuous world as a single parent and divorce was never your desire. However, you were thrust into this struggle by the choices of another. Someone else may have made decisions that currently dictate your situation, but that person cannot dictate your identity. Others cannot dictate the kind of person you will choose to be in your situation.

Resolve to rise above situations others may have forced on you, to be the person you want to be. It is commonly said, that "hurting people hurt people." You may have been hurt by someone else, but you aren't required to pass hurt along. With God's help, choose not to be a conduit of their pain. Choose to be a healthy response to it.

> *You may have been hurt by someone else, but you aren't required to pass hurt along. With God's help, choose not to be a conduit of their pain. Choose to be a healthy response to it.*

People may be able to force on you what you will have to live through, but they cannot force on you who and how you will choose to be. Follow Joseph's Biblical example to gain this power over what has been done to you.

Second, *choose to forgive them.* Forgiveness is NOT acting like the event didn't happen. Forgiveness doesn't mean they "got away with it." Forgiveness doesn't mean you have to have a relationship with them and act like nothing happened. Indeed, it is possible and may even be advisable to forgive some people and yet have no relationship with them. Forgiveness is choosing to no longer hold an offense against someone; you simply choose to cease to foster resentment for what has been done. In some cases of major life hurts, getting to such a place of forgiveness may require the help of a trusted friend, pastor or counselor.

Keep in mind that forgiveness is a process not an event. Just as we can re-experience the pain of injustice inflicted on us, we often need to re-release offenders from their sins against us.

At the end of the book of Genesis after Jacob and his family were reunited in Egypt, he modeled one of the greatest examples of forgiveness in all human history. (The full story is worth reading in chapters 42-50)

As we might imagine, now that Jacob had died, Joseph's brothers were appropriately afraid: *"When Joseph's brothers saw that their father was dead, they said, 'What if Joseph should bear a grudge against us and pay us back in full for all the wrong which we did to him!'"* (Genesis 50: 15).

When his brothers fell on their faces in fear before him, Joseph replied as only someone who had chosen to forgive his offenders could do: *"...Do not be afraid for am I in God's place?*

And as for you, you meant evil against me, but God meant it for good to bring about this present result to preserve many people alive. So therefore, do not be afraid..." (Genesis 50: 19, 20).

Keep in mind that forgiveness is a process not an event. Just as we can re-experience the pain of injustice inflicted on us, we often need to re-release offenders from their sins against us.

Joseph's response reminds us of a truth that is repeated throughout scripture, a truth that makes forgiving (and forgetting) easier. The truth is quoted in Romans 12: 19

"Vengeance is mine, I will repay, says the Lord." When we have been severely wronged, we don't need to become obsessed with "settling the score" or making sure they "get what they deserve."

While there is a time for accountability and retribution may be appropriate in many situations, some of the greatest sins to forgive (and forget) are the ones people seem to "get away with." In times like these, remember God is just and leave score-settling up to Him whenever and however He sees fit. Joseph did, and by the time his brothers fearfully apologized, God had healed his heart and blessed him past their offenses...it just didn't matter anymore.

Joseph also models a strong trust in the wisdom and workings of God which made forgiving his brothers possible. *"You meant evil against me, but God meant it for good..."* (Genesis 50: 20). Trust that God is aware of and involved in even the worst of your situations. As Psalm 46:1 tells us *"God is a very present help in trouble."* Rest assured, God is with you. God is present in your time of trouble; He sees what has happened, and He cares.

 Not only is He present, He is at work in your situation. Place your confidence in the truth *"God causes all things to work together for good, for those who love God, for those who are called according to His purpose."* (Romans 8: 28)

Believing in these truths makes letting go of the offenses of others possible. When we know God is with us and working for our good, we can let go of the wrongdoing of others knowing God will prevail and we can trust Him to "settle the score."

Third, *learn to let go of what is behind, so you can move ahead.* The apostle Paul encouraged this when he wrote: *Forgetting what lies behind and reaching forward to what lies ahead, I press on..."* (Philippians 3: 13, 14).

Imagine how unpleasant Joseph would have been if he held on to the horrible thing his brothers did to him. At the very least, he would have been angry, sarcastic, untrusting and bitter. Surely, he would not have been a desirable candidate to oversee Potiphar's household. Angry bitterness would have consumed any opportunity to be chief among prisoners in the jail. Likewise, if he were a stream of sarcasm, Joseph would not have been a likely candidate for promotion within Pharaoh's government.

Joseph chose not to repeat his brother's offenses. Joseph chose to let go of what happened to him. No one is saying this process is easy or short, but with God's ongoing help, it can be done.

You don't need to be obsessed with what has unjustly happened to you. You don't need to define yourself by how you've been hurt. You don't need to give control of your inner world by living as a reaction to "them." If Joseph can overcome what his brothers did to him, you can overcome too.

With God's help, you can decide that you will NOT repeat your past. You can decide to grant forgiveness as often as needed, to whomever you need to forgive. This is as much for YOUR sake as theirs. You can let go of the things that happened that you didn't deserve, so you can lay hold of the good things God has in store for you.

With God's help and your own resolve, you can be like Joseph. With your ongoing dependence on God you no longer need to let what they did control you or your sense of well-being.

QUESTIONS FROM THE LIFE OF JOSEPH:

1. What are some of the painful emotions Joseph would have felt from the time his brothers seized him to the time he was sold into slavery and then the thirteen years he spent without his freedom?

2. What did Joseph's brothers expect him to do to them when they appeared before him after their father had died? Why?

3. What offenses are difficult for you to get beyond? How do they negatively impact you? If you could "forgive and (learn to) forget," how would it help you?

NOTES, THOUGHTS AND INSIGHTS:

CHAPTER FIVE: Lessons from the life of Deborah. Somebody needs to 'man up' for God and you might just be the woman to do it. You can follow God beyond gender (or other) stereotypes of the.

The Bible tells us in Genesis 1: 27 that God created mankind, both male and female, in His image. Eve was designed as Adam's helpmate; their relationship was mutually valuing and supportive.

With the fall of mankind, both genders suffered consequences and inter-relational strife began that continues between people to this day. A review of the Bible reveals that God continues to value men and women as created in His image. Part of our

> Deborah is an example of a woman who went beyond gender roles and stereotypical expectations of her day to be used by God in a history-making way.

fallen-ness is revealed in a competitive human tendency to de-value others in favor of ourselves. As such, many Biblical instructions focus on proper, unselfish and loving treatment of others.

The fallenness of humanity can be seen in how people treat each other: a lack of respect, poor valuing of others, being taken advantage of, and abuse are all evidence. Such devaluing can happen between people of different generations, different people groups and skin colors, and between the sexes!

Women often feel hindered by traditional roles and societal expectations. While certain gender related roles in society are common and healthy (valuing the nurturing nature of mothers or the stabilizing impact of a father in a home) some can be limiting to a woman's potential.

Deborah is an example of a woman who went beyond gender roles and stereotypical expectations of her day to be used by God in a history-making way. Learn the courage and creative risk-taking availability Deborah modeled in her walk with God. It enabled Him to use her in ways God may be wanting to use you too.

Lessons from the life of Deborah.

"Now Deborah sent and summoned Barak the son of Abinoam from Kedesh-naphtali, and said to him, 'Behold, the Lord, the God of Israel, has commanded, 'Go and march to Mount Tabor, and take with you ten thousand men from the sons of Naphtali and from the sons of Zebulun,

And I will draw out to you Sisera, the commander of Jabin's army, with his chariots and his many troops to the river Kishon; and I will give him into your hand.'

Then Barak said to her, 'if you will go with me, then I will go; but if you will not go with me, I will not go.'

And she said, 'I will surely go with you; nevertheless, the honor shall not be yours on the journey that you are about to take, for the Lord will sell Sisera into the hands of a woman.' Then Deborah arose and went with Barak to Kedesh." (Judges 4: 6-9).

In the ancient Middle East, men typically held the positions of governmental and military leadership. The Bible celebrates an exception to this in the story of Deborah. She was an exceptional leader who rose to the occasion and led admirably at a time of urgent need in her nation. Deborah remains an affirmation to women of their value and the

> *Deborah is an affirmation to women of their value and the meaningful purposes God intends for them, even beyond what might be typically expected. God is not a typical God.*

meaningful purposes God intends for them, even beyond what might be typically expected. God is not a typical god.

The book of Judges records a time in Israel's history when they had no king. Being kingless was by design. God had intended for ancient Israel to be a theocracy. God would be their King and He intended for Judges to serve and interpret His laws in everyday life. Sadly, this theological and governmental design failed miserably due to Israel's failed obedience.

This is cited in Judges 17: 6 and 21: 25:

"In those days there was no king in Israel; every man did what was right in his own eyes..."

A study of history affirms that this individualized ethic is always a recipe for societal disaster. The book of Judges records the tension between a God who prescribed both personal and societal laws to live by, and a people bent on doing their own will. Each time Israel strayed from God, blessings and protection that resulted from following His code of ethics also ceased. Israel would enter a season of painful consequences to their lawless living, and they eventually call out in repentance to God. God would then hear their cries and forgive their sins. As Israel returned to God's ways, blessings followed obedience. They lived in peace and righteousness until they were once again distracted to live by "what was right in each one's eyes" and the moral roller-coaster cycle repeated itself.

Sadly, the people of Israel fell into moral and spiritual compromise soon after Joshua led them into the "promised land." Each tribe failed to drive out the inhabitants of Canaan as God had instructed. As Israel settled into compromise, they did not pass along their faith and devotion to the next generation. Instead, they went after the gods of the land and lived according to the sinful customs of the people they were supposed to drive out. (See Judges 1, 2) God's divine rationale for a thorough conquest and driving out of the inhabitants was validated as the Israelites succumbed to the immoral "culture creep" of the foreigners among them.

> *The book of Judges records the tension between a God who prescribed both personal and societal laws to live by, and a people bent on doing their own will.*

The story of Deborah happened more than 120 years into this period of the Judges during the downturn of one such cycle: *"Then the sons of Israel again did evil in the sight of the Lord...And the Lord sold them into the hand of Jabin king of Canaan...and he oppressed Israel severely for twenty years..."* (Judges 4: 1-3).

As our story begins, Deborah had already distinguished herself as a godly woman of good judgment and discernment with the spiritual gift of prophecy: *"Now Deborah, a prophetess, the wife of Lappidoth, was judging Israel at that time..."* (Judges 4: 4).

Deborah received a "word from the Lord" that He was going to deliver Jabin's army into Israel's hands in military victory and defeat Jabin's commander, Sisera. She summoned a man named Barak to commission him for the divine order. Barak sensed the danger inherent in this plan and insisted he would only go if Deborah accompanied him.

His request seemed somewhat superstitious as though Deborah was a sort of spiritual-military "good luck charm" as well as cowardly and unbelieving. He had more fear than faith. Deborah cooperated with his request, but not before making it clear that if she went with him to battle, she would end up getting credit for the victory not Barak:

"Nevertheless, the honor shall not be yours on the journey that you are about to take, for the Lord will sell Sisera into the hands of a woman." (Judges 4: 9).

Judges 4: 11-17 records the striking military victory by Israel led by Deborah and Barak. As Sisera the commander of the enemy army fled for safety, another female hero rose to the occasion. Sisera came to the nomadic tent of Jael, the wife of Heber the Kenite. There was peace between King Jabin and the Kenites, so Sisera assumed this family would be an ally and place of refuge. He couldn't have been more wrong.

Jael agreed to hide Sisera under a rug in the back of the tent. She hid him, gave him a bottle of milk to drink, and he drifted off to sleep, exhausted and battle weary. Jael then *"took a tent peg and seized a hammer in her hand and went and secretly drove the peg into his temple, and it went through into the ground..."* (Judges 4: 21).

The next chapter of Judges is devoted entirely to a song of victory. The song was composed and sung by Deborah and Barak. Four times Deborah was celebrated in this song as a heroic leader of the armies of Israel. Barak was mentioned but only as one who accompanied Deborah into battle. This affirmed Deborah's warning that she, not Barak, would get the credit for the victory. Further in the song, Jael was also celebrated as the warrior-woman who took the life of Sisera the enemy commander.

The story of Deborah and Jael is a timeless example of how God uses women. In this case, it appears no godly men could be found for the task who were courageous enough. Deborah was already being used in the spiritual gift of prophecy. According to the need of the moment, Deborah also became a military leader. Jael responded to an unexpected opportunity and struck the final blow for victory over the kingdom of Jabin.

> *However, God looked beyond gender-oriented expectations and met the need. It appears God's greatest criteria for a task at hand is not previous experience, not our gender, but our availability.*

God uses women. In the desperate example of the times of Barak, someone needed to "man up" and deliver Israel from the armies of Jabin, King of Canaan, it seems Deborah was the only person willing to do so. God used another woman, Jael, to complete the victory. This had to be an unlikely turn of events. Women were not typically seen in governmental or military leadership. However, God looked beyond gender-oriented expectations and met the need. It appears God's greatest criteria for a task at hand is not previous experience, not our gender, but our availability.

How about you? Do you limit yourself to stereotypical expectations?

Far too often people don't rise to an occasion to meet a challenge or fill a need because they or others don't believe they meet expectations. Perhaps you are the same; perhaps you have seen a need but told yourself "I can't do that!" Deborah might challenge your thinking and have you ask yourself, "Why not?" Some people bring societal stereotypical thinking to the work and ways of God. They assume "I couldn't do it because…I'm female, I don't have that experience, I'm male, I'm too young, too old, I don't have that talent, I can't afford it" …the list is endless.

We can learn a few lessons from Deborah and Jael.

First, *Deborah displays an understanding of God that goes beyond cultural stereotypes. Cultural norms don't dictate divine attitudes and expectations.* She did not put God in a box, or limit who He was or how He dealt with people. I recall a story told by a missionary years ago. The missionary told of a conversation with a woman who had heard the stories of the Bible and concluded, "Surely your God must be a woman."

From a western mindset this might seem like a curious observation. However, the woman speaking to the missionary was from a "third-world" country that treated women like second class citizens. This woman saw that women featured throughout scripture were respected, celebrated and valued.

Examples of a high Biblical esteem for women abound. This is seen in Proverbs 31 or in the birth narrative of Jesus where Elizabeth and Mary are among the Bible's greatest heroes and examples of righteousness. The Apostle Paul exhorts us that we are *"all one in Christ"* regardless of being male or female and regardless of racial or economic background (Galatians 3: 28, 29).

The story of Deborah isn't necessarily a call to change all of society's roles and expectations, but it does serve as a valuable reminder that cultural norms don't dictate divine attitudes.

This is not to say the Bible doesn't see and value the differences between male and female. However, it cannot be stressed enough that from the very first chapter of scripture, "female" is an equally celebrated dimension of being created in the image of God:

> *"And God created man in His own image, in the image of God He created Him; male and female He created them. And God blessed them; and God said to them, 'Be fruitful and multiply, and fill the earth, and subdue it; and rule over the fish of the sea and over the birds of the sky, and over every living thing that moves on the earth...'*

And God saw that all that He had made,
and behold, it was very good."
(Genesis 1: 27, 28, 31).

The story of Deborah illustrates God's value of women. In two chapters (Judges 4,5) there are two heroes, and both are women. The ancient Middle Eastern cultural context surrounding this story is not unlike today. Men sat in the primary seats of governmental and military leadership and still do. The story of Deborah isn't necessarily a call to change all of society's roles and expectations, but it does serve as a valuable reminder that cultural norms don't dictate divine attitudes.

Second, *Deborah was willing to step into roles typically occupied by men, when God directed her, even if it was unexpected or uncomfortable.* Deborah was willing to serve in a man's world when a man wouldn't. "Girls don't do that" was not a hindering expectation. What drove Deborah was not the expectations of others, but "what is God leading me to do?" Deborah seized the God-directed moment and prevailed.

> *Too many women today have silenced God's song in their hearts. Too many fail to live authentically in the way and as the person God has called them to be.*

For women reading this, don't be limited by "What would another woman do about this?" Rather, let your consideration be "What is God leading me to do about this? Regardless of my gender and surrounding expectations of me as a woman?" If God has empowered you, and God lays a need on your heart, consider that God is calling you to action and respond!

Third, *Sing and be true to the song that God has placed in your heart.* Define and live out your femaleness in the context of your relationship with the One who made you a female! Listen to the words of Deborah's song as she celebrates the song fulfilled in her obedience:

"I Deborah, arose... I arose, a mother in Israel...Awake, awake, Deborah, Awake, awake, sing a song!" (Judges 5: 7, 12)

Too many women today have silenced God's song in their hearts. Too many fail to live authentically in the way and as the person God has called them to be because it doesn't meet stereotypical expectations or identities others have of them. Dare to be different; Deborah did, and her courage has been recorded and celebrated for over 3,000 years! Define your expectations on yourself as a woman in the context of your relationship with the God who designed and destined you to be a female.

God has formed you, gifted, shaped and equipped you. Refuse to yield to the insecurity that cripples so many women (men too). See yourself as a woman created in God's image. See yourself as a woman created by a God who created you on purpose, for a purpose. That purpose is to serve, honor and obey him in big and small ways. If you've been stifled by stereotypes or immobilized by insecurity, resolve to get started following, obeying, and walking in the confidence of the one who made you in His image.

QUESTIONS FROM THE LIFE OF DEBORAH:

1. God created people, both male and female in His image. How does God intend for us to value and celebrate gender differences? Why does there seem to be competition or divisiveness between them instead?

2. Barak was too fearful to obey God's original prophetic word communicated through Deborah (that he should lead the people to victory.) Still, he was courageous enough to accompany Deborah, and humble enough to accept her victorious leadership. What positive lessons can we learn from Deborah and Barak's relationship?

NOTES, THOUGHTS AND INSIGHTS:

CHAPTER SIX: Lessons from the life of Josiah. Never underestimate the impact of a child.

In previous generations a familiar statement was "Children should be seen and not heard." Such thought clearly shows a diminutive attitude toward the value of a child and the wonders of childhood. This is contrary to the attitudes of Jesus who raised the importance of children when he contradicted a crowd who wanted to keep kids away from Him: *"Permit the children to come to me; do not hinder them, for the kingdom of God belongs to such as these."* (Mark 10: 14).

> *It comes as no surprise then, that children and youth play a major role in Biblical history.*

The Bible maintains the value of children. Psalm 127: 3 tells us that *"Children are a gift from the Lord, the fruit of the womb is a reward."* It comes as no surprise then, that children and youth play a major role in Biblical history. As a teenager, Joseph began an unlikely journey that led to a position of royalty in the ancient Egyptian empire. David killed Goliath as a teen and sung of slaying wild beasts as at a tender age. Mary and Joseph played a key role in the birth of Christ, most likely around the age they would have qualified for a modern-day driver's license.

One of the greatest spiritual and political reformers in the history of ancient Israel began his reign as king when he was only eight years old. His name was Josiah. We have much to learn about the divine value and intentions of youth from the life of Josiah, the child-king who transformed a nation.

Lessons from the life of Josiah.

> *"Josiah was eight years old when he became*
> *king, and he reigned thirty-one years in*
> *Jerusalem; and his mother's name was*
> *Jedidah the daughter of Adaiah of Bozkath.*
>
> *And he did right in the sight of the Lord and*
> *walked in all the way of his father David,*
> *nor did he turn aside to the right or to the*
> *left..."*   (2 Kings 22: 1, 2).

Even though ancient kings often became kings early, eight years old is a very young age to ascend to the throne of any nation. Modern election-oriented politics finds eight-year-old kings unthinkable. True, no eight-year-old has the emotional, mental or physical maturity to lead a nation, but ancient governments weren't led by elections, they were led by monarchies achieved by either inheritance or military conquest. Being king was a

> *The kingdom Josiah*
> *inherited was a*
> *politically turbulent,*
> *morally fallen and*
> *spiritually bankrupt*
> *kingdom.*

family affair; kings received their throne from their dad once they died. If the child wasn't old enough to reign, family members and other advisors stepped in to sustain them as a puppet king until maturity enabled them to govern on their own.

Such was the case for Josiah, his first true apparently self-motivated act of transformational leadership didn't happen until the age of sixteen when *"he began to seek the God of his father David..."* (2 Chronicles 34: 3). It isn't totally clear who advised young Josiah until that time. Likely candidates include his mother Jedidah. She would have been queen under his father, and until Josiah took a wife. The prophetess Huldah provided spiritual guidance to young Josiah. Hilkiah the priest certainly provided some assistance to the young king as a counselor and an advisor. Each of them were key influencers in the brief records of Josiah's reign.

The kingdom Josiah inherited was a politically turbulent, morally fallen and spiritually bankrupt kingdom. Josiah's father Amon was assassinated when he was only 24 years old after two short years as king.

> *"And Amon did evil in the sight of the Lord as Manasseh his father had done, and Amon sacrificed to all the carved images which his father Manasseh had made, and he served them.*
>
> *Moreover, he did not humble himself before the Lord as his father Manasseh had done, but Amon multiplied guilt.*
>
> *Finally, his servants conspired against him and put him to death in his own house. But the people of the land killed all the conspirators against King Amon, and the people of the land made Josiah his son king in his place."* (2 Chronicles 33: 22-24).

There are three milestones in Josiah's life. The FIRST milestone was when he was crowned king at eight years of age by loyal followers throughout the kingdom of Israel who wanted to preserve the royal bloodline of the monarchy. As mentioned earlier, the SECOND was when Josiah was sixteen years old, *"he began to seek the God of his father David."* (2 Chronicles 34: 3). Attentive readers will quickly notice apparent genealogical inconsistency in this verse. David was not Josiah's biological father; he was his grandfather many generations removed. Josiah's father was Amon,

> *On this occasion of a personal spiritual and moral awakening at the age of sixteen, Josiah put his heart change into action. He began a kingdom-wide purging of the pagan idolatry that his father and grandfather had promoted throughout Israel.*

and his grandfather Manasseh was perhaps the most evil king of all Israel's history. Manasseh did repent later in his life and turn from his evil ways, but the moral and spiritual damage he did to Israel leading up to his repentance was horrendous.

In ancient cultures and many of today's non-western cultures ancestry remains a significant part of a person's identity. As such, a grandfather and other ancestor can be generically cited as a person's "father" especially in the sense of being a "spiritual father." This is the case in referring to David as Josiah's father, he truly followed the righteous "DNA" of his forefather David not his immediate father or grandfather.

On this occasion of a personal spiritual and moral awakening at the age of sixteen, Josiah put his heart change into action. He began a kingdom-wide purging of the pagan idolatry that his father and grandfather had promoted throughout Israel. He tore down altars, idols and various places of idol worship. He destroyed priests and cleansed the land of the many places that Israel practiced their spiritual rebellion. (2 Chronicles 34: 3-7).

The THIRD milestone in Josiah's reign happened when he was 26 in the eighteenth year of his reign (2 Kings 22: 3; 2 Chronicles 34: 8). At this time, the spiritually renewed and passionate young king sent officials to commission Hilkiah the high priest to begin the work of restoring the temple. The temple treasury was entrusted to Hilkiah to spend as necessary on the craftsmen and supplies needed for the project.

Hearing the long forgotten and neglected words of God's law, tender-hearted Josiah tore his clothes in grief and repentance. He summoned the entire nation to a public reading of God's word and led them in repentance for generations of neglect and disobedience.

This restoration project had *three* significant results. *First,* as expected, the temple was restored to its function and beauty. *Second,* in the building cleanout and rebuild, Hilkiah found the book of the Law (the writings of Moses). He had it delivered and read to young Josiah. Hearing the long forgotten and neglected words of God's law, tender-hearted Josiah tore his clothes in grief and repentance. He summoned the entire nation to a public reading of God's word and led them in repentance for generations of neglect and disobedience. *Third,* Josiah led the entire nation in recommitting themselves to an obedient, humble, covenant relationship and lifestyle before God:

> *"And the king stood by the pillar and made*
> *a covenant before the Lord, to walk after*
> *the Lord, and to keep His commandments*
> *and His testimonies and His statutes with all*
> *his heart and all his soul, to carry out the*
> *words of this covenant that were written in*
> *this book. And all the people entered into*
> *the covenant..."*   (2 Kings 23: 3).

After this national repentance and recommitment, there was still more cleaning up to do. Josiah directed Hilkiah to purge the temple of all its pagan remnants. A fortune in gold, silver and carved wooden artifacts of pagan worship remained but were removed from the temple and destroyed. Although these tools of pagan worship were valuable, Josiah wanted nothing to do with them. More practicing pagan priests were found, removed and destroyed. He also removed those who practiced false spirituality as mediums and psychics. Near the end of this unprecedented year of spiritual cleansing, King Josiah led the people to once again celebrate the Passover feast which is the signature spiritual ceremony of God's covenant with His chosen people Israel.

The prophetess Huldah told Josiah that because of his humility, repentance and passion to obey God and use his power for good, God would bless him. Josiah's thirty-one-year reign would be one of success and peace. While Israel had already sown irrevocable seeds of rebellion that required a just and consequential response, God spared Josiah from such reckoning.

God later imposed practical consequences on the nation of Israel because of generations of disobedience and rebellion; they were eventually conquered by the Babylonians and sent into exile. However, as prophesied, God blessed Josiah throughout the rest of his reign. This young king would serve until he was 39 years old. He died due to wounds from a battle against Egypt that he mistakenly entered, contrary to God's direction. Young Josiah holds a revered place in Biblical history:

> *"And before him there was no king like Josiah who turned to the Lord with all his heart and with all his soul and with all his might according to all the Law of Moses, nor did any like him arise after him"* (2 Kings 23: 25).

Josiah's childhood mentors and advisors included spiritual people who obviously instilled a sensitivity for God, that later resulted in him demonstrating an exemplary passion for God, His word and His ways. Josiah could have simply

> *Josiah could have simply repeated the transgenerational flow of dysfunction and ungodliness that was modeled by his father, grandfather, and his ancestors before them.*

repeated the transgenerational flow of dysfunction and ungodliness that was modeled by his father, his grandfather, and his ancestors before them.

Josiah could have easily said "I'm young. The damage is done, why bother?" He could have simply chosen to enjoy the rights and privileges of being king and live a life of self-serving luxury.

Sin and dysfunction run along family lines. Most people just experience the dysfunction of their family and pass it along to their children, and their children's children. Josiah refused to do so. He said "no" to what was before him and experienced personal repentance and renewal. Then, he refused to pass along more sin to Israel. Instead, he led the entire nation in repentance and passed along the opportunity for righteousness!

While it is surprising that such a young king could lead in a transformational way, perhaps Josiah's youth was more of an asset than an obstacle. Josiah modeled the power of sincere youth. At the time he encountered God's word, he hadn't already lived a life marred by immorality and spiritual neglect. The reforms he led were far reaching and thorough. Josiah was

> *While it is surprising that such a young king could lead in a transformational way, perhaps Josiah's youth was more of an asset than an obstacle.*

unlike his grandfather Manasseh who came to repentance and turned to God late in life after being captured and imprisoned by Assyria. While Manasseh led a partial reform of Israel, his efforts were almost "too little too late." Josiah's youth proved to be a blessing as his passion for reform persisted until it spread throughout entire country.

Josiah and those around him refused to discount him because of his youthfulness. Likewise, he was surrounded by enough optimism to believe that change was possible. Josiah and his "handlers" held onto the hope for the possibilities of God.

How about you? Do you acknowledge the potential impact of youth and the power of repentance and obedience?

I recall a quote a poet once said, "A man's youth is a strange and wonderful thing, and he never understands it for what it fully is, until it is gone from him forever." I don't know if I completely understood this quote when I first read it inside a Dan Fogelberg album when I was in my twenties. Since that decade is well behind me I am beginning to understand.

Being young is a wonderful season of life. Childhood is a time of fun, discovery and innocence. The world is full of new experiences and hopefully we are surrounded by love, support and the good intentions of loved ones. Adolescence is an extension of the simple pleasures of childhood. Today adolescence also includes the encroachments of technology, a growing sense of responsibility and a need for learning and clarifying our direction that will propel us into adulthood.

Contemporary childhood is changing in the sense that there is more to consume the time and attention of our children than ever before. There is an almost compulsive level of busyness in today's modern family. With the pervasive nature of technology and social media family and society are increasingly complicated and "being a kid" seems to have more potential pitfalls than in the past. It is not uncommon to hear from older adults that children are being forced to grow up too fast these days.

Regardless of time and culture, one truth seems to resonate across the centuries of civilization. We should never underestimate the value and potential of children and youth. The Bible is full of examples of young heroes. David was a teenager when he killed Goliath. It is likely Mary and Joseph were teenagers when Jesus was born. Jesus exhorted His followers to develop a "childlike" faith, and in this chapter, we see the courageous exploits of such faith in a child-become-king.

> *Regardless of time and culture, one truth seems to resonate across the centuries of civilization. We should never underestimate the value and potential of children and*

Most people will acknowledge that they believe in the potential of youth. Yet they betray their inconsistency in spending (wasting?) all their parental or adult influence and attention by focusing themselves on developing their child's abilities to kick a ball, run, throw, catch, block or cheer at athletic or recreational activities. How might the stories of young biblical heroes be different if they had the obsessions of today's youth recreation surrounding them? Would David have been one of the most creative poets (Psalmists) in history if his youth was filled with video games and hand-held screen time?

The word recreation is self-explanatory; it comes from "re-creation." It literally means "the act of creating anew."[3] Recreational activities are meant to be some pastime that serves as a relaxing or fun diversion for replenishment and enjoyment. It is meant to accompany a life of purpose; it is not meant to become life's purpose.

> *Would David have been one of the most creative poets in history if his youth was filled with video games and hand-held screen time?*

Perhaps today's adults put their kids in all kinds of "fun" and athletic activities not only to meet incessant peer pressure of our times but also because we unknowingly underestimate the potential impact our children and youth can have now and in the future. Wise adults will value and prayerfully develop the potential of the children in their lives and families well beyond the athletic field and scheduled recreational activities.

Who knows? Your child, properly influenced, may be used of God to lead a cultural transformation someday. Perhaps they will make a major discovery, launch an incredible non-profit organization that addresses currently unmet

---

[3] Dictionary.com

human needs, or discover the cure for a debilitating illness. The list goes on.

Be certain the way you end up spending evenings, weekends and lots of family finances aligns with the long-term purpose God wants to shape in and through your child. Be sure to spend irreplaceable one-on-one relational time with your child that equips them for the intangibles in their future: marriage, family and work

> *Be certain the way you end up spending evenings, weekends and lots of family finances aligns with the long-term purpose God wants to shape in and through your child.*

relationships, a sense of competence and self-worth, a work ethic and personal responsibility, a love for God, His word, His ways and a love for others.

We can learn a few lessons from the life of Josiah.

First: *One of the most important lessons we learn from Josiah's life is his desire to obey God's word.* The power of such obedience is well stated in Holman's Bible commentary: "When God's people respond properly to God's word, God's spirit moves in renewing power."[4] The king commanded the temple be rebuilt. When God's Word was discovered among the rubble, Hilkiah the priest sent it to the king and had Shaphan the scribe read it to him. The king had an unusual transformational reaction to what he heard.

---

[4] Holman New Testament Commentary. WORDsearch11.

At twenty-six years of age, King Josiah heard laws of God that had been disregarded for generations. Realizing the disobedience of he and the nation of Israel, his heart was obviously heavy realizing how far they had strayed from obeying God's word. The king set out to remedy the disobedience of an entire nation. They renewed their covenant relationship and dependence on God, and God restored peace for Josiah for the next twelve years.

Beyond transforming the religious practices of Israel, the spiritual renewal led to practical reforms as well. The Bible says that *"Righteousness exalts a nation..."* (Proverbs 14: 34). As Josiah and other reformers throughout Biblical history brought God's people back to a place of humble obedience, the practical blessings of obedience typically followed. If we find ourselves living in disobedience to God's word, our humble repentance and return is typically met with God restoring and working in our lives.

What peace do you need restored in your life? Do things seem to be in disarray? Perhaps you're like ancient Israel and you've been neglecting the guidance of God's Word. Most of the time we don't intentionally disregard the Bible, we simply get distracted or sometimes disillusioned by life, and we drift. Model Josiah's humility. Repent, dive into God's Word, if possible, find people to do it with you, and start the kind of "search and replace" efforts Josiah did. What needs to stop being part of your life? What needs to start? Or perhaps it's not a matter of eliminating things from your life, but simply rearranging your priorities.

Second: *Recognize the importance of youth around you. Nurture the courage, determination, strength and potential of your children,*

> *Who in your life could use some encouragement?*

grandchildren and other youth in your life. God used more than immediate family members to influence Josiah. In addition to Josiah's mom Jedidah, the high priest Hilkiah, Shaphan the scribe and Huldah the prophetess all spoke constructively into Josiah's life at a young age. He learned the value of wise counsel and excelled beyond his years because of their influence.

Who in your life could use some encouragement? So often, young people are caught in a race for approval and popularity, and just feeling valued by you could be a refreshing, transformational influence. In addition, you could be the motivational "wind beneath their wings" to see their potential beyond a sports field or recreational activity.

Third: *If your family tree is damaged or undesirable, you are not bound to repeat inherited dysfunction.* Young Josiah demonstrated an encouraging truth. While immediate family influence is strong and sometimes seemingly inescapable, this young king lived out the possibility of not repeating the sinful trajectory of the generations that come before us. You too can do the same.

Your path to resisting and overcoming generational dysfunction and sin will be like Josiah. You must identify the sinful, painful ways those inherited traits that were modeled for you. Repent of them, resolve that with God's help you'll not repeat them. Tear down any family relics that help repeat the past. For example, perhaps a person fighting a history of alcoholism needs to clear the home of any alcohol, or a fight against repeating a father's pornography usage may require cancelling internet service so as not to be tempted to the same sin, etc.

> *Even though you may have wasted years in distraction or detour, God still has a plan for this season of your life. Resolve today to find it, to humble yourself and to seek Him in a fresh*

Seek God for spiritual vitality and renewal in your own life. Practical overcoming of negative traits is typically an outgrowth of inner restoration and renewal.

Fourth: *The story of Josiah causes us to wonder, "How many adults are simply grown up youth who are stuck?"* You should refuse to be a grownup who stays stuck in the consequences of past decisions. As an adult, are you living in disobedience and distance toward God that you should have returned from long ago? Resolve today to return to the youthful passion, innocence and optimism about God. Even though you may have wasted years in distraction or detour, God still has a plan for this season of your life. Resolve today to find it, to humble yourself and to seek Him in a fresh new way.

Perhaps you are like an uncle of mine. He had a successful business with his partner. They had all the material evidences of success, yet long after he retired he acknowledged, "I'm not certain I did the right thing, letting my eighteen-year-old self decide what I was going to do with the rest of my life."

> *To be realistic, there are many situations in life that we can't totally "undo." However, it can still be valuable to reconsider where you are, how you got there, and if there is anything you can alter now that would make a positive difference moving forward?*

In other words, he was successful, and raised a loving family, but couldn't silence the subtle question of whether he should have followed a life path different than the one he chose soon out of high school. Perhaps you find yourself on a life path that isn't rewarding in terms of what really seems to matter in God's eyes. Maybe you feel you're in the wrong career, or are spending your time, talent and resources in ways that don't mean the same thing to you now that they did then.

To be realistic, there are many situations in life that we can't totally undo. However, it can still be valuable to reconsider where you are, how you got there, and if there is anything you can alter now that would make a positive difference moving forward?

At times, we can miss it when it comes to God's ideal path for our lives. We can choose an educational or career path that wasn't His ideal. Perhaps even our mate choice wasn't the best, or where we chose to live, the list of possible ways we might miss God's ideal will for us goes on.

The Bible is full of examples of people who may have missed God's "plan A" but found that God knows how to make great "contingency plans." If this feels like it applies to you, spend earnest time in prayer. Humble yourself, if necessary, repent for not listening to God's voice in earlier years, rededicate yourself to Him, and trust Him to direct your paths from this time forward. Proverbs 3: 5-7 isn't a "once when you're young or else you're done" verse. Read the passage below, prayerfully recommit your ways to Him, and see how He directs your paths today from this day forward:

> *"Trust in the Lord with all your heart, and do not lean on your own understanding. In all your ways acknowledge Him, and He will make your paths straight. Do not be wise in your own eyes, Fear the Lord and turn away from evil..."* (Proverbs 3: 5-7).

QUESTIONS FROM THE LIFE OF JOSIAH:

1. No one is ready to be king of a nation at only eight
    years of age. How important were young Josiah's
    advisors and in what ways do you think they must have
    influenced him?

2. How do adults unintentionally underestimate or limit
    the potential impact of today's children and youth?

3. If Josiah could overcome the sins of his family before
    him and NOT repeat past sins and dysfunction, God
    can help you as well. What do you need to ask God to
    help you not repeat nor pass along in your family tree?

4. Can you cite an example from your life when you may
    have missed God's "plan A" but He blessed you with
    "Plan B?" (Do you need to ask God for a "Plan B" in
    your life today?)

NOTES, THOUGHTS AND INSIGHTS:

CHAPTER SEVEN: Lessons from Heaven. Just knowing you are going to Heaven can improve your life now.

Motivation is a key to making the most of our future. However, motivation can be difficult to find. Looking back can discourage us; in some seasons of life, looking ahead can be

> *Learn to pay more attention to Heaven, so you can pay less attention to the failures or pain of your past that hold you back.*

overwhelming. At times like this, it helps to look far into the distant future to find the help to overcome. When we know good things await us, the anticipation can propel us forward.

Your long-term heavenly future can help you overcome your past and make the most of tomorrow! In Heaven, regretful pasts are truly left behind. That which wounded, shamed us or held us back fades forever.

Guilt and shame are significant limitations to our sense of identity, worth and competence. This chapter examines how even the architecture of Heaven makes holding on to earthly shame an unnecessary hindrance.

Learn to pay more attention to Heaven, so you can pay less attention to the failures or pain of your past that hold you back. Heaven teaches us there is no ongoing justification for carrying around the emotional baggage of past pain, failure or insecurity

Once you learn from it, leave the past. Look back occasionally from a position of gratitude. Make the most of today and pursue God's dreams for the rest of your life. Always remember, Heaven is waiting for you!

Lessons from Heaven.

> "And I saw the holy city, the New Jerusalem, coming down out of Heaven from God...
>
> It had a great and high wall, with twelve gates, and at the gates twelve angels and names were written on them, which are those of the twelve tribes of the sons of Israel...
>
> And the wall of the city had twelve foundation stones, and on them were the twelve names of the twelve apostles of the Lamb..." (Revelation 21: 2, 12, 14).

This study has been focused on "Your best is yet to come, leveraging your past for a better future." We began with a review of Biblical perspectives on our past, present and future. We then considered examples of Biblical personalities who applied a Holy

Many Biblical heroes proved that past seasons of our lives certainly lead us to the next season, and with God's help we can change our direction. We can alter expectations; we can go a new path.

Spirit empowered approach to overcoming their past and building a better future. Many Biblical heroes proved that past seasons of our lives certainly lead us to the next, and with God's help we can change our direction. We can alter expectations; we can go a new path.

What has happened to us and the choices we have made certainly have an impact on us, but they need not bind us in hopelessness or failure. A painful, regretful or dysfunctional past does not need to totally ruin or predetermine our future. Our lives do not have to be a continual repeat of pain in the past or of the dysfunction in our family tree.

For those blessed in what is already behind them, a fruitful, productive past can propel us further in the future. However, past success is not a guarantee the future will be the same; many have known the unfortunate experience of things going wrong in a seemingly irrecoverable way after life was headed in a great direction.

Rather than looking back on our past and considering how we can leverage it for our future, this closing chapter looks ahead, and emphasizes that our ultimate destination in Heaven can help us make the most of our immediate future on this earth. Where we are going in the long run can help us maximize the next season in our lives.

First: *Let go of unnecessary guilt and shame before you get to Heaven and discover it doesn't matter anymore.* The Apostle John's book of Revelation ended with a scene from Heaven. He tried to describe this truly indescribable place; the best he could do was to create a sense of wonder and leave readers in anticipation, longing for the glorious paradise that is ahead.

John's brief, incomplete and somewhat cryptic description of "The New Jerusalem" can be a huge motivator for anyone trying to overcome past guilt. First, in the above passage from Revelation 21, notice the gates of the city. They are each named after the twelve tribes of the sons of Israel: Reuben, Simeon, Levi, Judah, Issachar, Zebulun, Joseph, Benjamin, Dan, Naphtali, Gad and Asher.

It may seem surprising that God would name the twelve gates of the city after these brothers. These are the names of the same jealous brothers who sold Joseph into slavery. The details of their individual branches of the Jacob family tree reveal that these men and their families were far from perfect. They became the twelve tribes of Israel and lived for generations in rebellion against God's covenant. Yet their names adorn the gates of the heavenly City.

One name on the gates of Heaven is curiously noteworthy, Judah. His name means "praise" and the tribe named after Judah reached Old Testament fame; yet their namesake (Judah) committed shameful sexual sin with his daughter-in-law Tamar

> *Letting go of unnecessary guilt and shame frees you to lay hold of the new seasons in your life that are yet to come.*

Although at the time, Tamar wore a face covering and Judah didn't know it was his daughter-in-law, he thought she was a prostitute.

Based on the architecture of Heaven, it is safe to say God doesn't remember our past sins! 1 Corinthians 13 tells us that love doesn't keep score of wrongs (vs. 5) and the gates of "The New Jerusalem" prove it! If God held on to our shame, He certainly would have omitted Judah from being the name of a gate of the holy city. In fact, it is doubtful that any of the heavenly gates would be named after the tribes of Israel. This validates the claim in Psalm 103: 12, *"As far as the east is from the west, so far has He removed our transgressions from us."*

To make the most of your future (until you get to Heaven) once you have asked God to forgive you. Learn to forgive yourself; God has. Letting go of unnecessary guilt and shame frees you to lay hold of the new seasons in your life that are yet to come.

While we should indeed rejoice over past blessings and good fortune, the Bible tells us that the reverse should also be true. Be joyful for the rest of your life knowing that the best of your life is yet to come...in Heaven!

Second: *Knowing that our earthly lives are finite, regardless of what is in your past, live each day like it is the gift from God that it is.* This attitude isn't a response to how things are going, or if life is turning out as we hoped, or whether people treat us well or not. Choosing to celebrate life as a gift is just that, a choice! Psalm 118: 24 says: *"This is the day which the Lord has made; Let us rejoice and be glad in it!"* Today, even as you read this book CHOOSE that you will rejoice. Philippians 4: 4 repeats this idea that joy is a choice, not a response to happy past or present situations: *"Rejoice in the Lord always, again I say rejoice."* The original Greek tense of the word means the word "rejoice" is in the imperative, and it is a command!

Jesus put this "rejoice-choice" in a heavenly context in Luke 10: 20: *"Nevertheless do not rejoice in this, that the spirits are subject to you, BUT REJOICE THAT YOUR NAMES ARE RECORDED IN HEAVEN."* Unfortunately, far too many people let their past indicate whether they will be joyful and rejoice. While we should indeed rejoice over past blessings and good fortune, the Bible tells us that the reverse should also be true. Be joyful for the rest of your life, knowing that the best of your life is yet to come...in Heaven!

Third: *Make decisions in your earthly future that will positively affect your heavenly one.* You are probably among most of us who have made decisions in your life that have had negative consequences on your future. Did you know that although decisions in your past may have damaged your earthly future, you can do things that will improve your eternal future?

> *Did you know that despite the way you've lived your past and damaged your future, you can do things that will improve your eternal future?*

The Bible speaks repeatedly of the fact that how we live in obedience to God on earth will someday be rewarded in Heaven. "For we must all appear before the Judgement Seat of Christ, that each one may be recompensed for his deeds in the body, according to what he has done, whether good or bad" (2 Corinthians 5: 10). Jesus often spoke about the importance of righteous, loving behavior noting "your reward in Heaven is great..." (Luke 6: 23; 35; Matthew 5: 12, etc.).

Indeed, we are saved by the amazing grace of God. There is nothing we can do to earn our salvation. However, this doesn't mean it doesn't matter how we live our lives. The Bible is also clear that as our salvation is a gift of grace. We will be rewarded for our obedient, Christ honoring behavior on earth when we get to Heaven (Ephesians 2: 10).

Below are a few passages of scripture that affirm the reality that how we live now and in our immediate future will be ultimately rewarded in our experience in Heaven:

> *"He who sows righteousness gets a true reward."* (Proverbs 11: 18).

> *"Do not lay up for yourselves treasures on earth, where moth and rust destroy, and where thieves break in and steal. But lay up for yourselves treasures in Heaven...for where your treasure is, there your heart will be also."* (Matthew 6: 19-21).

> *"And whoever in the name of a disciple gives to one of these little ones even a cup of cold water to drink, truly I say to you he shall not lose his reward."* (Matthew 10: 42).

> *"Well done, good and faithful servant, you were faithful with a few things, I will put you in charge of many things; enter into the joy of your master..."* (Parable of the talents) *(*Matthew 25: 14-4).

"Be glad in that day and leap for joy, for behold, your reward is great in Heaven." (Luke 6: 23).

"Now he who plants and he who waters are one; but each one will receive his own reward according to his own labor (for the cause of the Gospel)." 1 (Corinthians 3: 8).

"Watch yourselves that you do not lose what we have accomplished, but that you may receive a full reward." (2 John 1: 8).

What you decide to do FROM NOW ON in the immediate and extended future of your earthly life will make a difference in how you are rewarded in Heaven! No matter what it takes, whatever is in your past, DON'T let that hold you back from living the most heavenly rewardable life from this day forward!

> *What you decide to do FROM NOW ON in the immediate and extended future of your earthly life will make a difference in how you are rewarded in Heaven!*

With the understanding that "God is a God who rewards us" let your heavenly future help you make the most of your earthly future. Be sure to get started TODAY, and don't overcomplicate it. Jesus made it clear that even simple acts of kindness matter, even giving a cup of cold water to someone can be rewardable behavior. (Matthew 10: 42)

Fourth: *Many of us let past wounds in life damage our sense of self-worth, which in turn can harm how we live and relate to others in our future.* Looking ahead, let your heavenly self-esteem shape present feelings about yourself, and in turn, improve how you treat others, and how you treat yourself. *"Beloved, now we are children of God, and it has not appeared yet what we shall be. We know that, when He appears, **we shall be like Him**, because we shall see Him just as He is"* (1 John 3: 2).

> *No matter what it takes, whatever is in your past, DON'T let that hold you back from living the most heavenly rewardable life from this day forward!*

Someday in Heaven, we are going to be made perfect, in the likeness of Jesus Himself! This is almost unbelievable, but the Bible says it. Imagine, some day we will be as perfect as Jesus. Why then should you go around now, mentally beating yourself up for who you are or are not? Why carry around insecurities and inferiorities if indeed someday you will be made as perfect, as loving, kind and capable as Jesus? Not only are you a work in process, you are a work in process that is going to ultimately result in being complete and perfect in Christ. The words of Paul take on incredible encouraging significance: *"For I am confident of this very thing, that He who began a good*

work in you will perfect it until the day of Christ Jesus"
(Philippians 1: 6).

Stop letting the insecurities from your past continue to
hinder your future. Sometimes, you can't let go of your
past insecurities by looking behind you. Sometimes the best way to stop being insecure and inferior is to look ahead of you, to whom you will finally be in

> *Adjust your current self-esteem to be more in line with the person you are in the process of ultimately becoming.*

Heaven. Adjust your current self-esteem to be more in
line with the person you are in the process of ultimately
becoming.

Choose to feel better about yourself today because you
are in a process of refinement that God will bring to
completion in a perfect, heavenly version of you! When
you look in the mirror and are overwhelmed with who you
are NOT, remind yourself in the words of an old country
saying; "You ain't seen nothin' yet!"

Finally: *Develop a mindset of increasing growth and
fruitfulness now because that is what God has in store for
you in Heaven.* Surely when it comes to Heaven, most of us
have no adequate conception of what it is, or what it will
be like. This is reflected in the honest question, "But what
will we DO for eternity in Heaven?"

We have an inadequate idea that Heaven is just an endless
worship service with eternal songs that won't end. Either

that or we imagine some caricature of everyone floating blissfully around with angelic wings, playing harps (perhaps even playing in that eternal worship service, as if guitars must not have made it to heaven!)

Our minds fall short in our ability to conceive of such a marvelous place. The Apostle Paul references our cluelessness about Heaven: (1 Corinthians 2: 9).

> *"But just as it is written, Things which eye has not seen, and ear has not heard, and which have not entered the heart of man, all that God has prepared for those who love Him."*

Suffice it to say, Heaven is an amazing place. Keep in mind, Jesus calls it the "Kingdom of Heaven." There are over 100 such references in the Gospels to Heaven as a kingdom. Whatever we anticipate in this marvelous place that we will inhabit for eternity, we must think in terms of Heaven being a "Kingdom." Heaven is a divine society with the complex components of a culture that will still need governing and fulfilled responsibilities to function properly.

You and I, as redeemed saints of God, living eternally in His Kingdom, will serve Him. This is mentioned in Revelation 22: 3 as John describes his vision of Heaven and the throne of God: *"...and His bond servants shall serve Him."*

Heaven is a place where the curse has been removed from all God has made (Revelation 22: 3) but Heaven is not a place where God has discarded all His original creation principles and practices. There is no reason to assume that Heaven won't resemble anything of Earth or the original universe, it will just far surpass anything we have known due to Heaven's eternally unfallen nature.

As such, we can expect Heaven to be a society of beings interconnected relationally and spiritually. God will be personally present in Heaven and He will be the object of our worship and greatest attention. Yet there will be "coming and going" in Heaven (Revelation 21: 21-26), and there is an implied sense of purpose and responsibility for all citizens of Heaven.

> *Why in Heaven would we suddenly have no responsibility and no need for connectedness to one another in a place where such relationships would finally be free of our human deficiencies, codependence and dysfunction?*

Again, if one of the greatest dimensions of our earthly existence as Christians is to be individual members of the body of Christ and we all have spiritual gifts for the good of the body, why in Heaven would we all of a sudden have no responsibility and no need for connectedness to one another in a place where such relationships would finally be free of our human deficiencies, codependence and dysfunction? We should rightly expect a healthy (perfect) web of relational and purposeful interconnectedness with one another, and the divinely restored potential to fulfill it.

A societal view of Heaven puts Jesus' parable of the good steward in perspective in Matthew 25: 14-30:

> "...And the one who had received the five talents came up and brought five more talents, saying, 'Master, you entrusted five talents to me; see, I have gained five more talents.
>
> His master said to him, 'Well done, good and faithful slave' you were faithful with a few things, I will put you I charge of many things, enter into the joy of your master.'"

For this parable to speak to us about Heaven, we need to understand the symbolism behind it. Chapter 25 begins with Jesus trying to explain what Heaven is like: "Then the Kingdom of Heaven will be comparable to..." In the next verse He tells the famous parable of the ten virgins.

> The faithful servants who were responsible to their master's trust were rewarded with more responsibility in their master's kingdom.

Jesus begins the story of the good steward in verse 14 the same way: "For it (the Kingdom of Heaven) is just like a man about to go on a journey..." In this parable a rich master called His servants to Himself and charged them with responsibility while He went on a journey. The master entrusted resources to his servants, expecting them to maximize them to the best of their varying abilities and earn a profit he expected to collect when he returned. The master then returned and called each servant into account. The faithful servants who were responsible to their master's trust were rewarded with more responsibility in their master's kingdom. Those who were unfaithful were rejected with horrific consequence.

Jesus told this parable to explain Himself. He both commissioned and equipped his disciples (servants) as He left on a journey and will someday return and "settle accounts."

> "Are you living life with an attitude of opportunity now, knowing that you have more awaiting you in Heaven?"

The rest of the Gospels help us understand this parable. First, in Matthew 28: 19, 20 Jesus gave his followers the "Great Commission" to go into all the world and make disciples.

Second, He went on a journey to prepare a heavenly place for us, spoken of in John 14: 2, 3 *"For I go to prepare a place for you, and if I go to prepare a place for you, I will come again, and receive you to myself that where I am, there you may be also..."* Jesus made it clear that He would also return from His journey, that He would hold us accountable at the Judgement Seat of Christ (2 Corinthians 5: 10) and reward the diligent so that we could return to the Heaven He prepared for us.

We can surmise from this parable that tells us about Heaven ("For it is just like a man about to go on a journey") that Christ's faithful followers who lived productive lives for His sake, WILL BE BLESSED WITH A GREATER ROLE OF RESPONSIBILITY IN HEAVEN. This realization begs an important question. "Are you living life with an attitude of opportunity now, knowing that you have more awaiting you in Heaven?"

Live your life as a journey of discovery. Each day seek to discover how God has made you and equipped you, and what good work He has prepared for you to do. Then, do it passionately, knowing God sees and will reward your faithfulness.

> *From Jesus' perspective, this opportunity is seen as a reward for your earthly faithfulness and fruitfulness. In the economy of the Kingdom of Heaven, responsibility isn't a punishment it is a REWARD!*

Enthusiastically realize that someday your faithful fruitfulness will yield you greater opportunities (responsibilities) in the Kingdom of Heaven. In the economy of the Kingdom of Heaven, responsibility isn't a punishment it is a REWARD!

Do you see yourself now as a person with potential to do what matters for God? You are! Live life as a series of opportunities to be a good steward of the time, talent and opportunities God brings your way. Tell yourself, "God had given me abilities to use for His sake and will reward me for it! God sees me with potential!"

This encouraging attitude and approach to life now and for your immediate future is motivated and grounded in the reality of where you are headed! Heaven is a glorious, eternal kingdom without sin, shame or regret. Someday, not only will we get to live there for eternity, we get to help rule and reign there with Jesus! Now THAT understanding will make your tomorrows hopeful and purposeful!

QUESTIONS FROM OUR EVENTUAL HOME IN HEAVEN:

1. Knowing that the gates of the New Jerusalem are named after them, how do you suppose the twelve sons of Jacob would feel about God's ability to forgive and forget their shameful past failures?

2. How does the fact that you will be perfect (like Jesus) in Heaven encourage you despite your present imperfections?

3. What are some opportunities you could take to gain Heavenly rewards? What distracts you from pursuing them?

NOTES, THOUGHTS AND INSIGHTS:

A FINAL THOUGHT FOR NON-CHRISTIANS.

First, Thank you! Thanks for obtaining and reading this book. I trust at the very least it has helped you identify constructive and courageous attitudes and behaviors that you can apply in your life to leverage your past for a better future.

The people featured as examples in this book are real Bible personalities who lived at least 2,000 years ago. It's interesting to see how technology has changed through the centuries, but human nature is largely the same.

The Bible tells us that one thing we all have in common, is that we all tend to sin, and without God, our sin makes us spiritually lost.

This book has dealt a lot with making good decisions and behaving in a way that makes that decision good. We can't change our past, but we can choose how to live in response to it.

We can't personally undo our sins, but we can turn to Jesus who will forgive us for our sins and provide us the hope of Heaven. Please read and ponder the following verses.

According to these Biblical truths, every person needs to ask Jesus to be their Lord and Savior. If you haven't asked, you also need to be forgiven of your sins; Jesus is eager to forgive you, if you ask Him, and invite Him to be the Lord of your life.

"For all have sinned and fall short of the glory of God." (Romans 3: 23).

"For the wages of sin is death, but the free gift of God is eternal life in Christ Jesus our Lord" (Romans 6: 23).

"Jesus answered and said to him, 'Truly I say to you, unless one is born again, he cannot see the kingdom of God.'" (John 3: 3).

"For God so loved the world that He gave His only begotten Son, that whoever believes in Him shall not perish but have eternal life" (John 3: 16).

"But Christ demonstrated His own love toward us, in that while we were yet sinners, Christ died for us" (Romans 5: 8).

"If you confess with your mouth Jesus as Lord and believe in your heart that God raised Him from the dead, you shall be saved" (Romans 10: 9).

"If we confess our sins, He is faithful and just to forgive us our sins and to cleanse us from all unrighteousness" (Romans 1: 9).

"If anyone is in Christ, he is a new creature; the old things passed away; behold new things have come." (1 Corinthians 5: 17).

If you would like to ask Jesus to forgive you of your sins, and invite Him to be your Lord and savior, it is a decision of your mind, a desire of your heart, and a request from your mouth. You can begin this journey of knowing and following Christ with a simple prayer. An example for you to follow is provided below:

"Dear Jesus,

Thank you for dying on a cross to pay the spiritual penalty for my sins. I realize I need you. Please forgive me of my sins and become my Lord and Savior. If there are sins that are especially troubling you, feel free to confess them to God in prayer at this point.

I choose to place my trust in the fact that you died on a cross to save me not to condemn me. I also believe you conquered death and rose from the grave. I trust you will empower me to follow you with the help of your Holy Spirit. Someday, I will spend eternity in Heaven with you and all who chose to believe.

Thank you for loving me, for forgiving me, and receiving me today as a child of God.

I love you Jesus,

Amen.

Now that you have taken this step of faith, the Bible says that the angels in Heaven are rejoicing over you! (See Luke 15: 7) Pray daily, thanking God for his love and goodness, asking for Him to guide and direct your life.

Read the bible daily. Start perhaps by reading a chapter from the Gospel of John each day, and/or read the chapter from the book of Proverbs that corresponds to the day of the month (there are 31 chapters, if today is the 10th of the month, read chapter 10, etc.)

Finally, find a church to attend regularly that preaches the truth of the Bible and offers you opportunities to study with other Christians and to volunteer together in activities that help others.

God bless you!

P.S. This book originally accompanied a weekend sermon series (October/November 2018) at Christian Life Center in Dayton, Ohio. You may watch the series online, or if we can be of any spiritual help to you, please check out clcdayton.com

Made in the USA
Monee, IL
04 April 2021

63575519R00075